Bloom's Modern Critical Views

Bloom's Modern Critical Views

Mary Wollstonecraft
  Shelley
Percy Bysshe Shelley
Alexander
  Solzhenitsyn
Sophocles
John Steinbeck
Tom Stoppard
Jonathan Swift
Amy Tan
Alfred, Lord Tennyson

Henry David Thoreau
J. R. R. Tolkien
Leo Tolstoy
Ivan Turgenev
Mark Twain
John Updike
Kurt Vonnegut
Derek Walcott
Alice Walker
Robert Penn Warren
Eudora Welty

Edith Wharton
Walt Whitman
Oscar Wilde
Tennessee Williams
Thomas Wolfe
Tom Wolfe
Virginia Woolf
William Wordsworth
Richard Wright
William Butler Yeats

Bloom's Modern Critical Views

TRUMAN CAPOTE

Edited and with an introduction by
Harold Bloom
Sterling Professor of the Humanities
Yale University

CHELSEA HOUSE
PUBLISHERS
A Haights Cross Communications Company
Philadelphia

A Haights Cross Communications ✦ Company

Printed and bound in the United States of America
10 9 8 7 6 5 4 3 2 1

Library of Congress Cataloging-in-Publication Data

Truman Capote / edited and with an introduction by Harold Bloom.
    p. cm. -- (Bloom's modern critical views)
Includes bibliographical references and index.
  ISBN: 0-7910-7397-1
 1. Capote, Truman, 1924--Criticism and interpretation. I. Bloom,
Harold. II. Series.
  PS3505.A59 Z883 2002
  813'.54--dc21

                                        2002152059

Chelsea House Publishers
1974 Sproul Road, Suite 400
Broomall, PA 19008-0914

http://www.chelseahouse.com

Contributing Editor: Pamela Loos

Cover designed by Terry Mallon

Cover: Hulton-Deutsch Collection/CORBIS

Layout by EJB Publishing Services

Contents

Editor's Note

My introduction meditates upon Truman Capote's ambivalences toward literary tradition, and surmises that the self-curtailment of his later work emanates from his obsessive need to be his own "real progenitor."

Kenneth T. Reed begins the chronological sequence of criticism with his overview of *Other Voices, Other Rooms, The Grass Harp,* and *Breakfast at Tiffany's,* finding deep similarities between the three romances.

Capote's role as a pioneer of the nonfiction novel is analyzed by Robert Siegle, who employs the story *Handcarved Coffins* as his text.

In an admirable survey, Bruce Bawer considers Capote's entire career, and isolates the writer's tragic flaw as a refusal to transcend a narcissistic stance toward his own talent.

Blake Allmendinger trenchantly reveals the influence of Eudora Welty upon Capote, who denied all influences.

In Cold Blood, an ambiguous masterwork, is seen by Eric Heyne in the general context of literary nonfiction, after which Chris Anderson emphasizes how much even *In Cold Blood,* like the rest of Capote, relies upon reticence and ellipsis.

Early Capote is seen by Helen S. Garson as simultaneously evoking a transient youthful happiness and a darker melancholy that will devour it.

In Cold Blood then receives three very diverse accounts by Brian Conniff, Horst Tonn, and John Hollowell, all of whom however agree on the common element of the book's rather desperate quest for meaning.

In this volume's final essay, William White Tison Pugh returns us to Capote's starting-point, the Southern Gothic of *Other Voices, Other Rooms.*

Introduction

So many eminent authors have resented all intimations they ever were influenced by a forerunner, that Truman Capote's obsessive denials in this matter are remarkable only for their intensity.

In a later preface for a reprinting of *Other Voices, Other Rooms* (first published in 1948), Capote denied the palpable influence upon the book of William Faulkner, Eudora Welty, and Carson McCullers. They counted for little to him, Capote asserted, as compared to Henry James, Mark Twain, Poe, Willa Cather, and Hawthorne. Behind this odd grouping, one discerns Capote's quest to be self-generated: Poe and Cather made a difference to his art, but James, Twain, and Hawthorne all were very remote.

I read *Other Voices, Other Rooms* soon after it appeared, borrowing the novel from the current shelf at the Cornell University Library. I have just reread it for the first time since then, after more than a half-century. I remembered it surprisingly well, since it had seemed to me derivative, but the distinction of the prose was evident enough then, and remains lacquered enough now to preserve it in the mind. The closing paragraph can represent the high gloss of the style:

> His mind was absolutely clear. He was like a camera waiting for its subject to enter focus. The wall yellowed in the meticulous setting of the October sun, and the windows were rippling mirrors of cold, seasonal color. Beyond one, someone was watching him. All of him was dumb except his eyes. They knew. And it was Randolph's window. Gradually the blinding sunset drained from the glass, darkened, and it was as if snow were falling there, flakes shaping snow-eyes, hair: a face trembled like a white beautiful moth, smiled. She beckoned to him, shining and

silver, and he knew he must go: unafraid, not hesitating, he paused only at the garden's edge where, as though he'd forgotten something, he stopped and looked back at the bloomless, descending blue, at the boy he had left behind.

The Capote-like protagonist, still just a boy, enters the sexual realm with the transvestite Randolph, and looks back at the self left behind. This is not a study of the nostalgias or a lament for lost innocence. It is style for style's sake.

So rococo are *Other Voices, Other Rooms* and *Breakfast at Tiffany's*, that they remain something more than period pieces, though their preciosity makes it virtually impossible for me to venture prophecies as to their survival value. Try reading Capote side-by-side with Ronald Firbank, author of such sublime hilarities as *Valmouth*, *The Flower Beneath the Foot*, and *The Eccentricities of Cardinal Pirelli*. Compared to Firbank's blazing out-rageousness, early Capote fades away into pastel shades.

But there is another Truman Capote, who wrote *In Cold Blood*, still the most effective of "nonfiction novels." I reread *In Cold Blood* rarely and reluctantly, because it is both depressing and rhetorically very effective. The depression, as rereading makes clear, is caused by Capote's covert imaginative identification with the murderers, Perry Smith and Richard Hickock. Perry Smith is Capote's *daemon* or other self, and it is no surprise to learn that Capote cultivated the murderers, wept for them at the scaffold, and paid for their burials. Whether the cold, artful book deserves canonical status, I am uncertain, but it is likely enough to survive. It reflects its America, which is still our own.

KENNETH T. REED

Three Novel-Romances

Capote's longer narratives are, of course, open to different avenues of interpretation. One such avenue is as an expression of his own life experience, inasmuch as all of the longer pieces are not without their clear autobiographic side. But from a somewhat different point of view, the pieces are an outgrowth of his short fiction in both style and content. Of the three extended narratives, the first two—*Other Voices, Other Rooms* (1948) and *The Grass Harp* (1951)—rely upon the American South as setting. The third, *Breakfast at Tiffany's* (1958), is set in New York, the scene of about half of his short stories. The tenor of the three books is such that they are all well within the province of the "novel-romance," for as Ihab Hassan has written, all attempt successfully "to engage reality without being realistic."[1]

Other clear similarities exist between the longer and the shorter fiction. Capote's preferences in protagonists—usually young and invariably eccentric—prevail in a world that is both comic and sinister at the same time: innocent in some respects, corrupt in others. Withal, it can hardly be questioned that in the short stories lie the literary grist out of which the longer pieces were conceived and written. There is, moreover, a relationship between theme, image, and symbol that exists among all three books.

From *Truman Capote*. © 1981 by G. K. Hall & Co.

3

I OTHER VOICES, OTHER ROOMS

Professor William L. Nance has remarked that *Other Voices, Other Rooms* "is an almost unbelievably intricate book,"[2] a view emphatically not shared by Alberto Moravia who saw it as "extremely simple in scheme and plot."[3] It is intricate enough, in any case, to demand at least a repeated reading in order to look beneath the subtle but deceptively simple narrative that Capote published at the age of twenty-four. The overt action of the novel seems perhaps simple enough at a first glance: thirteen-year-old Joel Harrison Knox has come from New Orleans to Noon City en route to Skully's Landing where he expects to be reunited with his father, Ed Sansom, who has been missing from Joel's life for the past twelve years. Joel's divorced mother has just died, and he is responding to an invitation, ostensibly written by Sansom and conveyed to Joel's aunt and guardian Ellen Kendall in New Orleans. Sansom's letter proclaims that he is once again prepared to assume his "paternal duties, forsaken, lo, these many years," and that he can now provide Joel with "a beautiful home, healthful food, and a cultured atmosphere." Ellen Kendall has urged Joel to depart for Skully's Landing on the condition that he has the option of returning to his original home, should he become discontent. Joel senses, however, that his departure is a relief to her.

In Noon City Joel arranges a ride on a turpentine truck bound for Paradise Chapel, where he will need to make still other transportation arrangements to Skully's Landing; he completes the trip on a buggy driven by the seemingly ancient Jesus Fever, a Negro with a curved back and a face "like a black withered apple." The twelve-year-old twins Florabel and Idabel Thompkins hop aboard Jesus Fever's wagon also. Florabel has a girlish temperament but Idabel is so much a tomboy that she reminds Joel of "a beefy little roughneck" he had known in New Orleans.

Joel arrives in Skully's Landing asleep and is ushered sleepily to his quarters where he awakens the following morning in an "immense four-poster." From his bed he catches a first glimpse of his father's wife, Miss Amy, ominously killing a bluejay. There is a knock at his door, but instead of his father, it is Miss Amy, who gives him an oblique welcome, and explains that the house has neither electricity nor plumbing. She also tells Joel that "Cousin" Randolph, a "poor child" who suffers from asthma, was born in the bed in which Joel had slept, and that Angela Lee, Randolph's mother, had died there.

Joel makes repeated inquiry about his father, but he receives no information. He makes the acquaintance of Jesus Fever's niece Missouri, a young black servant girl who answers to the name "Zoo," and who tells Joel that at the age of fourteen "this mean buzzard name of Keg … did a crime to me and landed hisself in the chain gang." The crime, it turns out, was that Keg (Zoo's husband) succeeded in cutting her throat. Zoo is convinced that "Papadaddy [Jesus Fever] gonna outlive Methusaleh," but even so, "when he gone" she is "aimin' to light out for Washington D. C., or Boston, Coneckikut" so that she can fulfill her ambition of seeing snow. But although Joel and Zoo become friends, she admonishes him, "don't never ax me nothin bout Mister Sansom. Miss Amy the only one take care of him. Ax her."

Bored and confused, Joel decides to revert to a childhood diversion he calls Blackmail, "a kind of peeping-tom game he had known in New Orleans," where he had witnessed such baffling things as "a young girl waltzing stark naked to victrola music" and "two grown men standing in an ugly little room kissing each other." He looks up at the yellow walls of the house and wonders which of the top floor windows belong to him, his father, Cousin Randolph, and it is at this moment that he sees a "queer lady … holding aside the curtains … smiling and nodding at him, as if in greeting or approval." The queer "woman" is actually Randolph in sexual disguise, although Joel is not yet aware of "her" identity. When Joel asks Randolph about the woman at the window, he receives no answer. Instead, Randolph prefers to talk about the marriage of Keg and Zoo, and of Keg's cutting her throat. Joel asks once again "when am I going to see my dad," but Randolph's only answer is "when you are quite settled." Joel does, however, succeed in finding out about the Cloud Hotel, once "located in these very woods," and owned by Mrs. Jimmy Bob Cloud who, after a series of tragic deaths associated with the hotel, "went to St. Louis, rented herself a room, poured kerosene all over the bed, lay down and struck a match."

Joel discovers later on that it was Randolph, and not Edward Sansom, who had written Joel's letter of invitation to Ellen Kendall. But in a still more important discovery, he at least sees his father, who appears to him only as "a shaved head lying with invalid looseness on unsanitary pillows." Sansom is paralyzed and helpless, and his only means of communication is to drop tennis balls on the floor to attract attention. Following the realization of his father's condition, Joel accepts an invitation from the masculine Idabel to go fishing, where in turn she invites him to bathe naked in a creek. When Joel hesitates, she spits between her fingers and informs him that "what you've got in your britches is no news to me," and when he attempts to kiss her a few minutes later, she attacks him by pulling his hair and causing him to "cut his buttocks" in the scuffle that ensues.

With Randolph again, Joel learns the background of the whole set of bizarre circumstances into which he has been plunged. Randolph had been living in Europe for two years, copying paintings in museums, living with a woman named Dolores, and in love with a prize fighter named Pepe Alvarez, who was managed at that time by Ed Sansom. Apparently because of complications arising out of Sansom's "owning Pepe," Randolph has sent a bullet through Sansom's back, and sent him falling down a flight of stairs. In his agony, Sansom called for Joel, and meanwhile, Amy has come from Skully's Landing to play the role of nurse and wife. "Thus," says Randolph, "we all came back to the Landing; Amy's idea, and the only solution, for he would never be well again." These events, coincident with his mother's death, account for the position in which Joel now finds himself.

Jesus Fever dies and is placed in an unmarked grave beneath a moon tree. Zoo embarks on foot for points North, but soon returns, tragically, after having been raped by a white man and his four accomplices. Joel goes with Idabel to see the black hermit Little Sunshine who still lives in the dilapidated remains of the Cloud Hotel. On the way to the hotel, Joel kills a snake with Jesus Fever's war sword, but the two youngsters never complete their trip to Little Sunshine's. Instead, they come to a carnival where they meet the midget Miss Wisteria, a twenty-five-year-old "girl" who has "gold sausage curls" and a "pennyflute voice." Joel rides a Ferris wheel with her, at which time she runs her hand between his legs. A rainstorm interrupts the scene, blackening the carnival lights.

Joel falls ill, runs a fever, and dreams a vivid scenario involving all the persons who have played a part in his life. Upon his recovery, Randolph takes him to see Little Sunshine who, Randolph says, "wants to see us." But Little Sunshine had not, in fact, been expecting the pair, nor is he pleased to see them when they arrive. Randolph and Joel tie the mule, John Brown, to a spittoon and enter the Cloud Hotel where, shortly, the mule follows them upstairs. Soon, however, the animal "lunged, splintering [off of] the balcony's rail" and remained suspended by the neck in death. Randolph and Little Sunshine are by this time impossibly drunk. When morning dawns, it is "like a clean slate for any future." In an act of revelation, Joel climbs a tree and begins to see, among other things, the essence of his own identity: "I am me … I am Joel, we are the same people." He sees too that Randolph is "more paralyzed than Mr. Sansom." He then guides Randolph back to Scully's Landing where, in the book's final paragraph, he sees the queer woman once again in Randolph's window: "She beckoned to him … and he knew he must go," but he pauses momentarily to look back "at the boy he had left behind."

Other Voices, Other Rooms is, of course, open to various kinds of explanation, but probably the most imposing of these is as an initiation story. Capote makes it very clear during the development of the novel that his Joel Knox is one more on the lengthy list of essentially innocent American boy-men who appear so often in the pages of American literature from Mark Twain's Huckleberry Finn to J. D. Salinger's Holden Caulfield. Like Nathaniel Hawthorne's Robin in "My Kinsman, Major Molineux," Joel Knox is a naive young man who has left his home in search of better things: an improved living circumstance, and a father, who will pilot him through his difficult adolescent years. The development of *Other Voices, Other Rooms* is therefore partly to be measured in terms of Joel's gradual shedding of childhood innocence and his progressive movement toward maturity and a sense of personal identity.

When first seen in the novel, Joel appears "too pretty, too delicate and fair skinned," with an aura of "girlish tenderness" about him. Just as Robin carries a cudgel with him as a talisman, and as Holden Caulfield bears a red hunter's cap, Joel brings with him the wedding trip valise once used by his grandfather Major Knox, "a prominent figure in the Civil War." He bears also the spurious letter attributed to Edward R. Sansom with its promises of a better life for Joel. But the longer Joel travels, the more strange and perilous his journey becomes. His new Panama hat is stolen in the Biloxi railway depot, and after that, the bus to Paradise Chapel "had run three hot, sweaty hours behind schedule." Upon his arrival at Skully's Landing, Amy refers to him as a "poor child," and, like Hawthorne's Robin, Joel is referred to as a "shrewd youth." Still later, Miss Amy calls Joel "a wise, thrifty boy." Longing to come of age, Joel writes his friend Sammy Silverstein back in New Orleans that "out here a person old as us is a grown up person." In the woods with the tomboy Idabel, however, Joel's hoped-for maturity fails him. She tells him a bawdy joke: ("...so the farmer said: 'Sure she's a pretty baby; oughta be, after having been strained through a silk handkerchief,'") but Joel fails to comprehend. "Skip it, son," Idabel replies. "You're too young."

When Randolph delicately informs him of the "grotesque quadruplets" (Randolph, Dolores, Pepe, and Sansom), and of the dangerous love quadrangle that has developed, Joel is taught a new lesson in life. Randolph tells him that "any love is natural and beautiful that lies within a person's nature," and that "only hypocrites would hold a man responsible for what he loves...." About to give Joel Papadaddy's sword, Zoo hesitates, for fear that Joel is still "not man enough for to own it." But the gift is bestowed anyway, and Joel uses it to kill the snake that threatens Idabel and himself during their journey to find Little Sunshine at the Cloud Hotel. Along with those other initiates in American literature, Joel decides that he is going to return to a less threatening way of life he had once known, but he learns that he can't go home again. At the carnival he notes that even that "darling little girl" Miss Wisteria weeps because "little boys must grow tall." He knows too that his Aunt Ellen was relieved to see him go, and that in spite of her offer to have him back for holidays (or for good, if he were discontent), she has, in fact, "never answered his letters." It is in his understanding of such circumstances as these that Joel accepts his destiny and moves in the direction of Randolph, the "she" who beckons to him from a window on the novel's final page. By this time Joel has indeed left the boy in him behind.

The novel can, of course, be read in other ways. As in James Joyce's *Ulysses*, there is the son quite openly in search of a father. Here, Joel's discovery of his father is an ironic, even ludicrous, letdown; for Joel no sooner comes to know his father (to the extent that this debilitated figure can be known) than he resolves to leave him and run off with Idabel. Toward the beginning of the book, Capote forthrightly underscores young Joel's ostensible "mission" by stating that "he was trying to locate his father, that was the long and short of it." On his arrival at Skully's Landing, Joel wonders how he should at last greet the father he has never known: "And what should he say: hellow, Dad, Father, Mr. Sansom? Howdyado, hello? Hug, or shake hands, or kiss?" Surveying the "impressive oak doors," Joel wonders later "which of them, if opened, might lead to his father." Fantasizing, Joel tells one of his numerous lies when he writes Sammy Silverstein that "you would like my dad," when in reality Joel has never seen him. He realizes later, still not having "met" his father, that "here no father claimed him." But as Robin meets his kinsman Molineux in tar and feathers, Joel eventually finds Ed Sansom ("poor Eddie, absolutely helpless") to be scarcely a human image. He later regrets ever having seen Ed Sansom, and feels a sense of guilt. Sansom, he thinks, "was not his father," but instead "nobody but a pair of crazy eyes." It is on the occasion of his abortive decision to leave the Landing that he places Sansom's hand against his own cheek and acknowledges the blood kinship between them, whispering "my only father."

Joel's initiatory experiences in the novel are also connected to his "identity" problems, as Capote makes quite clear. "Somewhere along the line," the narrative reads, "he'd been played a mean trick. Only he didn't know who or what to blame. He felt separated, without identity, a stone-boy mounted on a rotted stump...." But at the end of the book when Joel scales a tree, he goes "right to the top," spreading his arms to "claim the world" and proclaim loudly "I am me." There can be no doubt that he has discovered himself and has, in a kind of Joycean epiphany, managed to see, for the first time, the meaning of his world and his destined place in it. His comprehension of these crucial matters comes, symbolically as well as literally, through his journey from New Orleans to Skully's Landing—a peregrination into his own deeper consciousness—which, like the journey undertaken in Joseph Conrad's *Heart of Darkness*, leads into dark, psychic penetration.

Other Voices, Other Rooms is less a novel than it is a gothic romance: brooding, sinister, mysterious, inward-reaching, lyrical, and shadowy. The only sense of reality in it is psychological realism. The book is also a fine specimen of southern regional fiction, conveying as it does the flavor of backwoods life with its "steaming ... fried eggs and grits, sopping rich with sausage gravy," its overt racism (expressed, but not condoned), its sense of historical heritage (as stated, for example, in the tale of "a fiendish Yankee bandit who rode a silver-grey horse and wore a velvet cloak stained scarlet with the blood of southern womanhood"). Capote, however, once denied the book's sense of place: "I don't think that *Other Voices, Other Rooms* can be called a southern novel ... everything in it has double meanings—it could as well have been set in Timbuctu or Brooklyn, except for certain physical descriptions."[4]

Part of the intricacy of the book is Capote's ingenious and varied use of certain leitmotifs and image patterns. Perhaps central among these is the consciousness of death and dying, as intimated in the name "Skully." Not only has Joel's mother died just prior to the time the narrative begins, but her passing is the first of a series; Jesus Fever soon dies, as does his mule, John Brown, that Joel witnesses hanging from the balcony of the Cloud Hotel: "swinging in mid-air, his big lamplike eyes, lit by torch's blaze, were golden with death's impossible face, the figure in the fire." Joel learns too, of the Creole boy who, in 1893, "having taken a dare to dive into the lake from a hundred foot oak, crushed his head like a shell between two sunken logs," and of the gambler who swam out into the same body of water and never returned. He is aware also of Mrs. Jimmy Bob Cloud who had immolated herself in St. Louis. The flash of Zoo's gold tooth reminds Joel of the neon sign heralding "R. R. Oliver's Funeral Estb." where his mother's body had been taken. "At thirteen," in fact, "Joel was nearer a knowledge of death than in any year to come."

As in his shorter fiction, Capote was again attracted by the grotesqueness he recognized in life, a grotesqueness that appears often in the course of Joel Knox's education. On first seeing Jesus Fever slumped atop his wagon, Joel notices the face that looks to him like a black withered apple and the "sickle-curved posture that made him look as though his back were broken." There are other suggestions of grotesqueness, as well. Miss Amy, Joel observes, has "a vague suggestion of a mustache fuzzing her upper lip." Idabel claims later on that she used to shave Randolph's late mother Angela Lee. Later, at the interrupted carnival scene, however, Joel and Idabel pay ten cents to view a stuffed chicken with four legs, as well as a "two headed baby floating in a glass tank like a green octopus." They also encounter The Duck Boy who, with webbed fingers, opens his shirt "to reveal a white feathery chest." The midget Miss Wisteria, dressed in purple silk, sings songs and recites poems through "rouged, Kewpie-doll lips." She has also a "pale, enameled face" and "hands [that] flitted so about that they seemed to have a separate life of their own." *Other Voices, Other Rooms* is not limited to such prospects as these, for the entire milieu of Skully's Landing is fraught with grotesque distortion. Even at the beginning, Sam Radcliffe, driver of the turpentine truck, finds Joel himself offensive because "he had his notions of what a 'real' boy should be like, and this kid somehow offended them." Joel's appearance and manner, however, are scarcely any match for Randolph's appearances in feminine disguise.

Capote makes extensive use of other images besides grotesqueness, one of these being the image of heat and fire. It is, for example, a "sizzling day in June" when Joel Knox appears in Paradise Chapel on his way to Noon City. After his arrival there, he makes connections with Jesus Fever (who later succumbs to the fever that Joel seems to have contracted near the end of the book). At Skully's Landing, Joel learns from Miss Amy that the dining room, music room, library, and porch have all been destroyed by fire sometime in the past. Still later, he hears about Mrs. Jimmy Bob Cloud who has voluntarily set fire to herself, and about Zoo's having been raped on her way to Washington, D.C., and having been tortured by a lit cigar driven into her navel. With Randolph at Little Sunshine's place in the Cloud Hotel the whole scene is illuminated by firelight.

There are a number of references to the sun, as suggested vaguely in the name "Sansom" and directly in the name "Little Sunshine." At the conclusion of the book, Joel looks skyward and sees images in the clouds. When they pass, he sees also that for him "Mr. Sansom was the sun. He looked down." Earlier he has recalled reading a textbook that informed him "that the earth at one time was probably a white hot sphere, like the sun."

Such heat imagery finds its counterpoint in the chilliness of cold soft drinks, beer, and watermelon. Just prior to his death, Jesus Fever suffers from chills that prompt him to cry out, "How come you let me freeze this away? Fix the fire, child, it's colder'n a well-bottom." Coldness, however, is mostly to be associated with death, and Joel's not infrequent references to snow, as

Professor Nance has pointed out, are to be identified with Joel's late mother.[5] That mental association is made reasonably clear in Joel's apocryphal story told to Zoo: "We were lost in the mountains, Mother and me, and snow, tons and tons of it, was piling up all around us. And we lived in an ice-cold cave for a solid week, and we kept slapping each other to stay awake: if you fall asleep in snow, chances are you'll never see the light of day again."

Capote's concern with animal imagery, however, is as apparent as his concern with images of heat and frigidity. Back in Paradise Chapel, Miss Roberta, proprietress of R. V. Lacey's Princely Palace, has "long ape-like arms that were covered with dark fuzz." At "home" in Skully's Landing, Joel is aware of the sinister "Judas vine [that] snaked up" the white fluted columns of the house, while "a yellow tabby cat was sharpening its claws." Still later, Joel makes the acquaintance of Zoo, the black woman who informs him of Randolph's liking for dead birds, "the kinds with pretty feathers." Joel gradually becomes conscious of the animal life around him: the mules, chicken hawks, lizards, snakes, hunting dogs, the "big Persian cat" that "sucked away all [the] breath" of a black infant, the buzzards, ants, and butterflies that inhabit the mysterious world of Skully's Landing.

There are still other motifs and images that weave the fabric of the book together. The bullet that Joel Knox steals from Sam Radcliff during the ride from Paradise Chapel to Noon City reappears in Joel's feverish dream near the end of the narrative. The Dr. Pepper and NEHI advertising signs that Joel sees on Paradise Chapel Highway, as well as the inscription on Idabel's shirt ("DRINK COCA-COLA") are echoed in the carnival scene when Joel rushes to ask Miss Wisteria if she might not join him and Idabel for a "sodapop." And the valise that Joel carries, the one that his grandfather had "used on his wedding trip around the world" recalls Randolph's later description of the "honeymoon" of Keg and Zoo which has ended in his cutting her throat. Furthermore, the story of the rape and murder of the three "exquisite sisters" by "a fiendish Yankee bandit," prefigures Zoo's rape and torture late in the narrative.

Particularly imposing are Capote's knife images that appear throughout the text. On one occasion, for example, Idabel brandishes a jacknife with "a thin vicious blade" before Joel's eyes, while she comments threateningly, "I could kill somebody, couldn't I?" as she stabs murderously into the side of a watermelon. There is perhaps an ironic outcome to Joel's prayer which asks God for "a knife with seven blades," for later Zoo gives Jesus Fever's sword to Joel ("This here was Papadaddy's proudest thing") which he straps to his waist and uses eventually to kill a snake. Joel is, of course, aware of Keg's knife attack on Zoo, but he is also aware of certain inevitabilities in human life later on when he notes that (in the case of Miss Wisteria) "there would always be this journey through dying rooms until some lovely day she found her hidden one, the smiter with the knife."

That *Other Voices, Other Rooms* is heavily autobiographic is perhaps clear enough to preclude any precise documentation. Involving, as it does, a young man's search for a home, a father, and a sense of identity, the book is created out of the patterns that prevailed in Capote's early personal history, although not necessarily to the letter. Although the book might conceivably be looked upon as an exercise in Capote's quest for self-understanding, that approach to the narrative is beyond the purview of this study. In 1956, Capote remarked that "last summer I read my novel *Other Voices, Other Rooms* for the first time since it was published eight years ago, and it was quite as though I were reading something by a stranger. The truth is, I am a stranger to that book; the person who wrote it seems to have so little in common with my present self."[6] Evidently because of the book's very controversial reception (as noted in Chapter 1) and the extent to which its author had invested himself in its pages, Capote seemed to want the whole episode in his career put well behind him.

II THE GRASS HARP

Again in *The Grass Harp*, Capote constructed a southern tale around a boy whose parents are deceased and who, as a consequence, goes to live with relatives. The relatives this time are two somewhat eccentric maiden sisters, Verena and Dolly Talbo. *The Grass Harp* is a great deal more elemental and witty than *Other Voices, Other Rooms*, and much less gothic in tone. The protagonist is the boy Collin Fenwick, to some extent another Capote self-portrait, eleven years of age when the story opens. His mother has died, and soon after his father, a seller of Frigidaires, has been fatally injured in an automobile accident. The older sister, Dolly, is Collin's favorite, and the two of them retire to the woods so that they can discover the natural ingredients necessary to concoct the dropsy remedy that Dolly prepares, bottles, and sells. But the younger sister, Verena, has an obsession with money, and is "the richest person in town" because of the drugstore, the drygoods store, the filling station, the grocery, and the office building that she owns. "The earning of it," says Collin, "had not made her an easy woman." Verena, Dolly, and Collin are cared for by a black woman named Catherine Creek who resembles Zoo in *Other Voices, Other Rooms*, and who claims to be an

Indian, although she is, in fact, "dark as the angels of Africa." Catherine refers to Dolly as "Dollylove," and to Verena as "That One."

When Dolly begins to earn enough from the manufacture of her dropsy remedy to pay income taxes, Verena begins to take a heightened interest in Dolly's enterprise. And when Collin reaches the age of sixteen, Verena embarks on a buying trip to Chicago and returns two weeks later with an enigmatic individual named Dr. Morris Ritz, "that little Jew" who "wore bow ties and sharp, jazzy suits," and who, according to Collin, "might have been a tap dancer or a soda jerk." At a dinner on Talbo Lane attended by Verena, Morris Ritz, Dolly, and Fenwick, Verena and Morris reveal the medicine bottles they have had printed, which read "Gipsy Queen Dropsy Cure." They also reveal their intention to apply to Washington for a copyright on the labels and a patent on the medicine. Dolly objects: "It won't do: because you haven't any right, Verena. Nor you, sir." Dolly is unaware, however, that Verena and Dr. Ritz are preparing to restore an old factory, and that Verena has given Ritz ten thousand dollars to furnish it with the machinery necessary to manufacture the medicine in marketable quantity.

Understandably unhappy, Dolly proposes that she, Catherine, and Collin venture out to a house built in a China tree some distance from Talbo Lane. Once situated in their arboreal home, they are joined by others as time goes on. The first to find and join them is a contemporary of Collin's named Riley Henderson, a fatherless son of a criminally insane mother. Verena, meanwhile, having found a note left by Dolly, goes to Sheriff Junius Candle and requests a search party to locate the three missing persons. From their tree house, the inhabitants look down to see "a distinguished party" approaching that includes Harvard-educated Judge Charlie Cool, the Reverend and Mrs. Buster, Mrs. Mary Wheeler, and Junius Candle himself with "a pistol flapping on his hip." Ordered by the preacher's wife to come down out of the tree, Dolly responds by asking Mrs. Buster to "consider a moment ... and ... realize that we are nearer to God than you—by several yards." Following that line of argument, Judge Cool says to Reverend Buster that perhaps "the Lord told these people to go live in a tree; you'll admit, at least, that He never told you to drag them out...." Following this, the judge himself joins the tree party, whereupon Collin remarks that "it was the judge who had most found his place in the tree."

On a later occasion, Sheriff Candle and his men return with a warrant of arrest signed by Verena who has accused them of theft. The three sheriff's deputies ("Big Eddie Stover was legally born a bastard; the other two made the grade on their own") begin to drag Catherine and slap her. Collin hits Eddie Stover in the face with a big catfish, while Catherine elbows and butts her way through the others, and is finally arrested for having struck Mrs. Buster with a Mason jar. It then develops that "Dr." Morris Ritz has suddenly left town, taking with him the contents of Verena's safe—twelve thousand dollars in negotiable bonds and more than eleven hundred dollars in cash. "But even that," Collin says, "was not half his loot."

A travelling family of evangelists, consisting of a woman and her fifteen children, comes to town and begins to promote one of their number, a twelve-year-old boy who wears steel-rimmed glasses and a ten-gallon hat, and looks, consequently, "like a walking mushroom." The homemade sign that the family brings with it reads "Let Little Homer Honey Lasso Your Soul For The Lord." The pathetic troupe come looking for Dolly Talbo, who eventually feeds the entire crew and gives them money. It is Reverend Buster, meanwhile, who applies to the sheriff for an injunction preventing Little Homer Honey from conducting any religious meetings, but the child does so anyway. People "who never dropped a dime in Buster's collection plate" now find themselves hanging dollar bills on "God's Washline," although the money is confiscated by "that puke-face Buster and what's-his-name, the sheriff: thinks he's King Kong."

A short time after their departure from the China tree, Dolly falls ill of the walking pneumonia and eventually dies of a stroke. Riley Henderson survives a bullet wound in the shoulder inflicted by Eddie Stover, and gets married. Collin serves as his best man, and lingers around the town a while "winning free beers on the pinball machine" but at last decides to pursue a degree in law. In the end, Collin strolls out into the September-burnished fields that had once surrounded the tree house. "I wanted then," says Collin, "for the Judge to hear what Dolly had told me: that it was a grass harp, gathering, telling, a harp of voices remembering a story. We listened."

As is true with *Other Voices, Other Rooms*, there are a number of points of view from which *The Grass Harp* can be examined to critical advantage. Reduced to its simplest terms, the book depicts the contending forces of conformity and social orthodoxy versus freedom and self-expression. The characters who best typify these differences in approach to living are Verena, who chases wealth; and Dolly, the older sister, who chases dreams. The remaining characters fall in to either of two categories; with Verena are Morris Ritz, the Reverend and Mrs. Buster, Mrs. Mary Wheeler, Sheriff Candle, and his deputies. With Dolly are the protagonist Collin Fenwick, Judge Charlie Cool, Catherine Creek, Riley Henderson, Sister Ida and her fifteen offspring ("Seems somehow I can't get on without another life kicking under my heart: feel so sluggish otherwise"). The contending that goes on in the book, over what are fundamentally questions of social conformity and self-reliance, is weighted in favor of the free-wheeling eccentrics and innocents who follow the way of Dolly Talbo. Consequently, the author's sympathies, predictably enough, are on the side of those who pursue their dreams: "A man who doesn't dream is like a man who doesn't sweat: he stores up a lot of poison" Judge Charlie Cool assures Verena, and his remark, as much as any single remark in the book, identifies its central theme. Earlier, Cool has referred to Dolly, Catherine, Riley, Collin, and himself as "five fools in a tree," but, he says, they are "free to find out who [they] truly are." If the five are not totally successful at unravelling the problem of self-recognition, they at least succeed in gaining some perspective on the world that lies below their tree house, a world which is by all odds less rational than their own.

The Grass Harp has other similarities with Other Voices, Other Rooms, for here is another local color story that makes much of the southern setting and its cultural aspects: diet, humor, a sense of place, and of history. Collin Fenwick, like Joel Knox, moves in the direction of self-knowledge and self-understanding which is achieved through a series of seriocomic incidents. Just as Joel Knox has triumphantly proclaimed his self-awareness from the heights of a tree, so too does Collin Fenwick come to terms with himself in a tree. Beyond the outward similarities, many of the leitmotifs are similar. There is, for example, some of the same kind of sexual reversal as in Other Voices, Other Rooms. The rumor once spread by Collin's father, "that Verena was a morphodyte," may have been exaggerated, but there are suggestions of her lack of sexual identity. In years past she has formed an attachment to Maudie Laura Murphy who worked in the local post office and who, to Verena's grief, ran away with a liquor salesman. Collin describes Verena as being "like a lone man," and Dolly discloses later that Verena was given to pipe-smoking. Verena eventually admits to Collin that she had loved Morris Ritz, but "not in a womanly way." And yet one of the last things that Collin says of Verena is that in her last years she has "grown feminine."

The preoccupation with death that had prevailed in Other Voices, Other Rooms, continues also in The Grass Harp. One of the first things to which the reader's attention is directed is the town graveyard containing not only Collin's mother and father, but twenty or so of his kinfolk. When Collin speaks of Carrie Wells, a schoolteacher who had toured Europe, he is reminded that the only things connecting his town with Europe are "the graves of soldierboys." Verena herself has expressed a desire to erect an imposing mausoleum to accommodate all of the Talbo family, and Judge Cool recalls with vividness his wife's dying in his arms. When Maud Riordan contemplates a Halloween party, she urges Collin to appear with "a skeleton voice." Judge Cool, when he vacates the home he had shared with his sons and their wives, rents a room at Miss Bell's boarding house which had only lately been transformed into a funeral parlor.

Another motif which ties the narrative together is the act of theft, a motif present in both *Other Voices, Other Rooms* and *Breakfast at Tiffany's* where the protagonist in each instance has inclinations toward petty thievery. But in *The Grass Harp* the idea of theft is emphasized heavily. Riley Henderson's uncle Horace Holton, it turns out, has been gradually draining the money belonging to his sister Rose. And when the treehouse party departs the house on Talbo Lane, "Catherine bragged that she'd robbed the pantry of everything, leaving not even a biscuit for That One's breakfast." Later, Verena swears out a warrant for the arrest of Catherine, Collin, and Dolly, on the grounds that they have "stolen property belonging to her." The only authentic theft in the novel, however, is Morris Ritz's cleaning-out of Verena's safe, although the sheriff's seizure of Sister Ida's revival meeting receipts seems tantamount to outright theft, as well. Verena herself, however, would have stolen Dolly's dropsy formula, if given the opportunity.

Capote uses the imagery of fish in various ingenious ways in the novel. Collin, at one point, recalls having kept tropical fish: "devils they were; ate each other up." Catherine, however, cherishes her goldfish that "fanned their tails through the portals of the coral castle" in their bowl. Riley Henderson, according to Collin, was both a good carpenter and a good fisherman. At one point, Collin suggests to Catherine that they abandon their tree and live aboard a houseboat owned by a man who makes his living "by catching catfish," but she declines the suggestion and insists upon living on land "where the Lord intended us." Somewhat later, Judge Cool suggests that the tree-dwellers "should taste my fried catfish sometime," and he recalls having caught a trout in his bare hand, just as Collin catches a huge catfish in the same manner. Up in their China tree, the inhabitants experience a driving rainstorm so severe that "fish could have swum through the air."

There is also the repetition of a kind of noose-imagery at certain points in *The Grass Harp*. Chapter Two, for example, opens in the woods when Riley Henderson comes into view, "and around his neck there hung a garland of bleeding squirrels." Collin himself has been hung similarly by Catherine earlier: "At fourteen," he recalls, "I was not much bigger than Biddy Skinner, and people told how he'd had offers from a circus." To remedy Collin's growth deficiency, Catherine pulls at his arms, legs, and head "as though it were an apple latched to an unyielding bough." When Charlie Cool first appears at the China tree, he unloosens from his vest a gold watch and chain, "then lassoed the chain to a strong twig above his head; it hung like a

Christmas ornament." On an earlier occasion, Verena berates her sister for her lack of enthusiasm over Morris Ritz's coming to dinner: "I'd appreciate it if you's hold up your head: it makes me dizzy, hanging like that." When Sister Ida and her fifteen assorted offspring arrive in town, it is her "Little Homer Honey" who will "Lasso Your Soul For The Lord." And in the midst of the controversy between Reverend Buster, the sheriff, and the occupants of the tree-dwelling, it is also Little Homer who does indeed lasso Reverend Buster, but not for the Lord. Little Homer's rope "dangled like a snake, the wide noose open as a pair of jaws, then fell, with an expert snap, around the neck of Reverend Buster, whose strangling outcry Little Homer stifled by giving the rope a mighty tug." Buster, "loose-limbed as a puppet," makes his way off the premises with the aid of several persons as Little Homer calls after him, "Hey, hand me back my rope!"

The Grass Harp is as much in the province of the romance as *Other Voices, Other Rooms*. To borrow the definition cited by Professor Hugh Holman, the romance "differs from the novel in being more freely the product of the author's imagination than the product of an effort to represent the actual world with verisimilitude."[7] In *The Grass Harp* the house built in a China tree, as well as the attic of the Talbo house (from which Collin looks thoughtfully down) are as removed from life on the bare soil as the book's overall removal from the starkness of unvarnished reality. The book itself is partly an illustration of the desirability of adhering to one's private, inner nature rather than yielding to the often hypocritical orthodoxy symbolized, for example, by the Reverend and Mrs. Buster. In his advocacy of adhering to one's inner dictates, Judge Cool says it best: "all private worlds are best, they are never vulgar places."

The quality of Capote's witty prose style is a point of emphasis in itself, quite apart from his use of theme and idea. Catherine's kitchen in the Talbo house, Collin says, is "warm as a cow's tongue." Sheriff Candle has fists "hard and hairy as coconuts." Elsewhere, Capote makes hilarious use of the outrageous and unexpected incident. Observing Riley Henderson urinate over a hill of red ants, Collin is "insulted" when Riley "switched around and peed on my shoe." Toward the end of the book, the reader is introduced to "the twice widowed Mamie Canfield" whose specialty is the early identification of pregnant women from the porch of her boardinghouse-funeral parlor: "Why waste money on a doctor?" one anonymous character is said to have asked his wife. "Just trot yourself past Miss Bell's: Mamie Canfield, she'll let the world know soon enough whether you is or ain't."

Unlike the generally critical reception of *Other Voices, Other Rooms*, the consensus of critical reaction to *The Grass Harp* was positive. Gene Baro, writing for the *New York Herald Tribune Book Review*, for example, proclaimed that "Truman Capote's literary stature seems now beyond question. His second novel, 'The Grass Harp,' supplements the undeniable achievement of 'Other Voices, Other Rooms.' Indeed, the present volume exhibits the maturing and mellowing of one of America's best young writers."[8] Oliver La Farge's review in the *Saturday Review of Literature* read, in part, "It is a real pleasure to see a young author coming along who possesses a change of pace; so many writers of all ages tend to carve eternally off the same joint, even after the meat has grown cold and dry, or even after there is nothing left but scraps. Variety within the broad range of his genre on the part of a writer as able as Truman Capote is something to welcome with cheers."[9]

III *Breakfast at Tiffany's*

No writer ever decisively breaks with the thematic and stylistic patterns of his work established over a period of years. *Breakfast at Tiffany's*, which appeared in 1958, seven years after the appearance of *The Grass Harp*, is not inconsistent with the kind of fiction Capote had been writing earlier. *Breakfast at Tiffany's* is a very chic, character-centered novella which is as frothy as it is enigmatic. Narrated in the first person, the tale is a personal story of one who relate the bizarre, somewhat fragmented incidents in the life of Holly Golightly to himself.

In technique, Capote drew upon some of the better features of his talent as a writer, relying as he did on elements of wit, irony of situation and language, lyricism, precision of feeling achieved through selectivity of detail, and an all-but-inexhaustible sense of satire. Capote's handling of wit is facilitated by the fact that Holly Golightly is one who quite literally lives by her wits. When, for example, she elects to evade an investigation of her supposed complicity in New York Mafia racketeering by an escape to Brazil, she makes a final outrageous request of the narrator: "Call up the *Times*, or whatever you call, and get a list of the fifty richest men in Brazil. I'm *not* kidding. The fifty richest: regardless of race or color." But the narrator disapproves of her plans to bolt the country and engage in Brazilian fortune-hunting while the police are looking for her in New York. "If they catch you jumping bail, they'll throw away the key. Even if you get away with it, you'll never be able to come home." But Holly has an answer for everything: "Well, so, tough titty. Anyway, home is where you feel at home. I'm still looking."

The book is virtually centered on a series of startling disclosures. Holly turns out to be not the "Miss Holiday Golightly, of the Boston Golightlys" as reported in a recent newspaper gossip column, but the former Lulamae Barnes, the runaway wife of Doc Golightly, a horse doctor from near Tulip, Texas. Golightly himself appears midway in the story: "... I bought myself a ticket on the Greyhound [from Texas]. Lulamae belongs home with her husband and churren." Holly, who has a proclivity for chewing her hair and for acts of petty theft ("I'd steal two bits off a dead man's eyes if I thought it would contribute to the day's enjoyment ..."), has been hired by a defrocked priest named Mr. Oliver O'Shaughnessy (who impersonates a lawyer) to visit convicted Mafia figure Sally (Salvatore) Tomato in jail every Thursday. At a meeting in Hamburg Heaven, O'Shaughnessy has asked Holly "how I'd like to cheer up a lonely old man, [and] at the same time pick up a hundred a week ... Well, I couldn't say no: it was too romantic." The whole idea, of which Holly seems incredulously unaware, is that Sally Tomato provides her with "verbally coded messages" having ostensibly to do with the weather, but which in reality are designed to permit Tomato (through Holly and O'Shaughnessy) "to keep first-hand control of a world-wide narcotics syndicate with outposts in Mexico, Cuba, Sicily, Tangier, Tehran and Dakar." If Holly is not entirely aware of her own acts, their meaning, and consequence, neither is the narrator, or for that matter, the reader.

The narrator himself relies on a number of sources for information about Holly. In addition to his attempts at sorting through her own oblique remarks, he talks to her conspicuously unattractive male friends, has conversations with bartenders, and looks at disclosures in newspapers. In spite of his inevitable inconclusiveness after this kind of investigation, he says, "I became ... rather an authority on [her]." In a particularly telling series of details, he relates his having rifled through the discarded odds and ends that make up her personal trash-basket. "I discovered," he says, "... that her regular reading consisted of tabloids and travel folders and astrological charts; that she smoked an esoteric cigarette called Picayunes; survived on cottage cheese and melba toast; that her vari-colored hair was somewhat self-induced. The same source made it evident that she received V-letters by the bale. They were always torn into strips like bookmarks. I used occassionally to pluck myself a bookmark in passing. *Remember* and *miss you* and *rain* and *please write* and *damn* and *goddamn* were the words that recurred most often on these slips; those, and *lonesome* and *love*."

These discarded artifacts of Holly's past life are projected into the larger fabric of the novella. It is in the city tabloids that her alleged social and criminal activities are exposed. The travel folders are emblematic of her restless spirit, and of the kind of life implied on the engraved card fitted into her apartment mailbox: *Miss Holiday Golightly, Traveling.* The astrological charts reveal something of the antirational, perverse, and unpredictable character of her life. They also confirm Holly's later remark that she has abandoned horoscopes, as she says, because they are a "bore." The Picayune cigarettes contain a hint about her somewhat mysterious and veiled southern origins. Her diet of cottage cheese and melba toast in part explains "all her chic thinness" and her "almost breakfast-cereal air of health" as evidenced by "a flat little bottom." Her hair coloring contains some indication of the deception with which her past and present life are clouded. But it is the V-letters written by service men that provide the best insight into her lonely and loveless existence. Torn as they are into slips that serve for bookmarks, the letters serve as a record of her unfulfilled, romantic dreams.

Holly, for all of the rumors and conjecture that surround her, is another example of an all-but-unassailable innocence. The narrator remembers her first as being ageless: "anywhere between sixteen and thirty." In reality, she is not yet nineteen, with "a face beyond childhood, yet this side of belonging to a woman." Her age and innocence are reminiscent of Kay in Capote's early story "A Tree of Night," who carries with her a green Western guitar into which she pours a glass of unwanted gin. Walking toward Joe Bell's bar, the narrator of *Breakfast at Tiffany's* bears with him what little Holly has left behind after her hurried departure for Brazil, and as he walks, Holly's abandoned guitar fills with rainwater. The innocence that Holly shares with Kay is in a way similar to the easy candor and outspoken bluntness observable in Miss Lily Jane Bobbit in "Children on Their Birthdays." The inscrutable D. J. in "The Headless Hawk" (another New York story) has in common with Holly a thoroughly unpredictable pattern of social behavior, along with a history of psychiatric treatment. What unites these characters is a paradoxically fortunate inability to shed the color and fantasy of childhood. As a consequence, they share a certain immunity from the tragic reality of life, an immunity characteristic of the prostitute Ottilie in the story "House of Flowers."

In the end, Holly makes good on her flight to Brazil, and then moves on to Argentina where she passes into oblivion. The last thing known about her destiny comes from an unlikely source (the Japanese photographer I. Y. Yunioshi), a former resident in Holly's brownstone in the East Seventies, who shows bartender Joe Bell three photographs taken in Africa of a black man "displaying in his hands an odd wood sculpture" which passes for "the spit-image of Holly Golightly." Yunioshi's investigations indicate that Holly, accompanied by two white men, had found their way to Tococul, "a village in the tangles of nowhere" where the two men had fallen victim to a fever and where Holly had allegedly "shared the woodcarver's mat." This is the last thing known about her. "All I hope," says Joe Bell, "I hope she's rich. She must be rich. You got to be rich to go mucking around in Africa." The only troublesome item that Holly (who wanted to "wake up some morning and have breakfast at Tiffany's") has left in New York is a cat with no name. Concluding two weeks of "after-work roaming through... Spanish Harlem streets," the narrator finds the nameless animal "flanked by potted plants and framed by clean lace curtains, ... seated in the window of a warm-looking room." Says the narrator, "I wondered what his name was, for I was certain he had one now, certain he'd arrived somewhere he belonged. African hut or whatever, I hope Holly has too."

Like the previous two novel-romances, *Breakfast at Tiffany's* can be read variously. Probably the most salient reading of the book is as a celebration of innocence and as a mirthful example of the short-circuiting of an essentially tragic and evil world, as symbolized by the wicked, ugly prospect of Manhattan and its inhabitants that forms the background for Lulamae, once the wife of Doc Golightly of Tulip, Texas. Although it is scarcely emphasized, the narrator's exposure to Holly has apparently been another step in his education as a writer of prose fiction. Toward the beginning of the book she asks him, quite undiplomatically, if he is a *real* writer. "It depends on what you mean by real," is his evasive response. "Well, darling, does anybody buy what you write?" she asks. "Not yet," is his reply. Later, he reads her a short story he has written; he notices that she fidgets, and that he "did not seem to have her interest." In the course of the book he manages to place some of his writing in a quarterly magazine, and on the final page of the book he discloses that he has sold two stories. It becomes gradually clear that it is Holly herself who has given him a subject worthy of writing about: herself.

Breakfast at Tiffany's shares with most of Capote's other fiction a concern for people who are liberated from the more commonplace moorings of social and cultural life, and who are scarcely concerned with such things as family relationships and middle class notions of respectability. To read *Breakfast at Tiffany's* is to become aware that the novelette itself is in part a deliberate affront to middle class respectability, consistency, dependability, and to the whole cluster of values that form the Protestant Ethic. When the narrator warns Holly that if she jumps bail, she will never again be able to come home, it impresses her not at all. Holly, like so many disengaged Capote characters, is decidedly outside the normally construed notions of value and reality. Holly prefers to be "natural" rather than "normal," and her manner of coping with the world makes her engaging not only to her author, but to the reader. She represents a certain independence of mind and freshness in her approach to manners and morals, albeit *Breakfast at Tiffany's* is not a particularly morally conscious book.

The consensus of reviewer's attitudes toward *Breakfast at Tiffany's* was almost uniformly high, and although no single review was noteworthy for its critical insight into the book, each of them found much to praise and virtually nothing to criticize negatively. Paul Levine, in the *Georgia Review*, made what is perhaps the most memorable comment about Capote and his new book when he remarked, "Like good whiskey (and unlike many of our one-shot novelists) Capote seems to improve with age."[10] Levine, like other followers of Capote, was by this time able to know what to expect from the author, and had identified a refinement in Capote's skill as a fiction writer.

Among the tendencies that might have been expected, for example, was a certain retrospective point of view in his fiction, and this point of view was again to prevail: "I am always drawn back to places where I have lived, the houses and neighborhoods," the narrator of *Breakfast at Tiffany's* remarks, "... there is a brownstone in the East Seventies where, during the early years of the war, I had my first New York apartment." That the narrator is once again to be closely identified with the author, perhaps goes without saying, for the narrator is, at this juncture in his career, a struggling writer of fiction whose work is mostly unsold and therefore unpublished. That Holly Golightly has provided him with something vital to write about means that she has inadvertently been a major force in his life and in his prospects as a writer. For the narrator, the end of the novelette is just the beginning. Holly is somewhere in Africa (perhaps). Sally Tomato has succumbed to heart failure at Sing Sing. Holly's former friends, the Trawlers, are now in the midst of divorce proceedings. But the narrator has managed to sell two more short stories and has vacated his brownstone apartment "because it was haunted." The ending of *Breakfast at Tiffany's* is not significantly different from the ending of *The Grass Harp* where the real center of the story is the impact it has on its narrator-protagonist: "a grass harp, gathering, telling, a harp of voices remembering a story."

NOTES

1. *Radical Innocence: Studies in the Contemporary American Novel* (Princeton, N.J., 1961), p. 244.

2. *The Worlds of Truman Capote* (New York, 1970), p. 63.

3. "Two American Writers," *Sewanee Review*, Summer, 1960, p. 478.

4. Roy Newquist, *Counterpoint* (Chicago, 1964), p. 80.

5. *The Worlds of Truman Capote*, p. 62.

6. Malcolm Cowley, (ed.) *Writers at Work: The Paris Review Interviews*, (New York, 1960), p. 290.

7. *A Handbook to Literature*, Third Edition, (New York and Indianapolis, 1972), p. 459.

8. "Truman Capote Matures and Mellows," *New York Herald Tribune Book Review*, Sept. 30, 1951, p. 4.

9. "Sunlit Gothic," *Saturday Review of Literature*, Oct. 20, 1951, p. 19.

10. *Georgia Review*, Fall, 1959, p. 350.

ROBERT SIEGLE

Capote's Handcarved Coffins *and the Nonfiction Novel*

T he nonfiction novel makes us uneasy by its apparently oxymoronic nature—its mixing of reality and fiction, of journalist and novelist, of factuality and imagination. Uncomfortable with so indiscrete a mixture, many writers on the subject resolve specific works back into either the novel or nonfiction. William L. Nance, for example, speaks of the "flaws" and "limitations ... inherent in the very concept of a nonfiction novel" and concludes that *In Cold Blood* "falls back into a category which may as well be labeled 'documentary novel.'"[1] In the most extended reflection on the type, Mas'ud Zavarzadeh shifts it in the opposite direction by calling it

> the "fiction" of the metaphysical void. In the absence of shared, preestablished norms, it maps the surrounding objectal world, without imposing a projected pattern of meaning on the neutral massiveness and amorphous identity of actual people and events. Its response to the confused and contradictory interpretations of reality, which are all the product of an Aristotelian compulsion to explain and label experience at all levels, is to return to noninterpretive, direct contact with actuality.[2]

From *Contemporary Literature* 25, no. 4 (Winter 1984). © 1984 by the Board of Regents of the University of Wisconsin System.

Zavarzadeh's ideal of objectivity—"direct contact with reality"—may be stated so extremely in order to contrast the type with the two principal alternatives he sees in contemporary fiction, the "liberal-humanist novel" (Bellow, Malamud, Updike), and "transfiction" (Barth, Pynchon, Barthelme), but he nonetheless argues that the "fictual" realm of the nonfiction novel has both the factual authority of reality and the "aesthetic control" of the fictional.[3] One side of the debate approaches the work in terms of its novelistic artistry, the other side in terms of its ability "to circumvent the intervening imposed interpretations and to return to the elementals."[4]

This curious split response can be explained by thinking of the "nonfiction novel" not as an oxymoron, but as a tautology. That is, works of this type bring us not up to a barrier between two distinct regions, nonfictional reality and fictional narrative, but into a vortex in which both kinds of accounts, together with the presumably metalinguistic commentary upon them, are drawn into the same discursive swirl. Each grounds itself by means of a figurative space, a literary triangle delegating specific zones to each, and allowing each to "cover" its limitations as discourse, as a way of knowing, by deferring elements of the "full picture" to the others—the way science defers matters of the heart to fiction, and fiction defers precise explanations of quantum mechanics to physics. Such strategy of differentiation seeks to stabalize each kind of discourse by suiting its method to its material. But part of the problem critics seem to have with the nonfiction novel is that nothing new or unique emerges from the "synthesis" of these supposedly distinct zones—not because it "falls back" into one or the other familiar kind, but because these kinds turn out to have been the same. Different methods all turn out to be varying conventions for framing, proportioning, and selecting from the same basic cultural myth of reality.[5] If such material is as much fiction as "reality," and if "method" is mainly convention—that is, fiction—then even the distinction of method and material turns out to be a version of the basic cultural logic from which all these illusory oppositions derive. They are, in other words, diacritical rather than independent variables.[6]

This redundancy in the nonfiction novel is the key to sorting out the anomalies readers find in it, and to look at Truman Capote's *Handcarved Coffins*—a brief and thus convenient piece for illustration—is to see how immediately useful this approach can be. In the preface to *Music for Chameleons*, the volume in which the story appears, Capote calls the book a "nonfiction short novel," and thus launches from outside the discourse of the narrative a presumably authoritative commentary upon it.[7] The rest of the document explains Capote's period of disorder after enraging critics with the publication of chapters from *Answered Prayers* in *Esquire*. Feeling himself "in a helluva lot of trouble," "suffering a creative crisis and a personal one at the same time," moving through a period of "creative chaos" that was "torment," Capote tells us he came to a new understanding "of the difference between what is true and what is *really* true" (p. xvi). The nonfiction novel, then, is the means of answering on both the personal and professional levels what amounts to the fundamental hermeneutical question, and *Handcarved Coffins* accordingly reproduces the hermeneutic investigator in the form of the sleuth and his scribe endeavoring to discover the truth and put it in writing.

This effort to establish the *"really* true" is the root of all cultural fictions. But as truth is a difficult goal at best, we had best return to Capote's preface to discover why and how he feels able to achieve it. There are curious aspects to the two basic ideas he advances at this point. Capote apparently considers the crisis in his writing as an unsatisfactory ratio between "the powers at my command" and "the total potential" of "all the energy and esthetic excitements that material contained" (p. xvii). If Nietzsche is right that "powers" are versions of a will to mastery over the materials of one's experience, then this passage presents the dramatic confrontation of order with the "energy" and "excitements" of its counterpart, the chaos of the material before the writer brings out of it the "total potential" of its truth. The dream of "total potential" or plenitude is not reached, however; for some reason the resources of writing cannot triumph totally over the recalcitrance of its material. We may at this point at least speculate as to why: if fiction and nonfiction, or perhaps even method and material, are no different, then such a triumph is impossible. It is like the dream of sign and referent merging, text and world, desire and fulfillment.

Capote remains buoyant, however. He exudes the ecstasy of desire for such a crossing, and bubbles with metaphors that command our attention. The "apparently unsolvable problem" he poses is this:

> how can a writer successfully combine within a single form—say the short story—all he knows about every other form of writing? For this was why my work was often insufficiently illuminated; the voltage was there, but by restricting myself to the techniques of whatever form I was working in, I was not using everything I knew about writing—all I'd learned from film scripts, reportage, poetry, the short story, novellas, the novel. A writer ought to have all his colors, all his abilities available on the same palette for mingling (and, in suitable instances, simultaneous application). (p. xvii)

It is no wonder that the work he returns to is *Answered Prayers*, for this wish amounts to the theological conception of fulfilling the inner truth of the spirit. Capote seeks to make his practice of writing as comprehensive as possible, absorbing into this application all the forms he has known, as if sheer range of generic conventions and techniques would achieve his dream of plenitude. The "voltage was there," it seems, although one cannot tell whether the voltage derives from the material as an inner truth to be brought out, or from Capote's earnestness despite his self-restrictions in technique. Perhaps it is enough to see, however, that the voltage raging through the material left the work "insufficiently illuminated," darkened in its partial order. If, somehow, an additional intensity of the light of order could be brought to bear upon the material, it would shine brightly with its "total potential." The truth is there; it needs illumination.

But strangely enough, as the paragraph moves towards Capote's own enlightenment, the metaphoric configuration shifts, and what the writer needs is not more light, but all his "colors" on "the same palette." His techniques now are an impasto smeared upon the canvas, covering what is there in order to portray on one surface the illusion of what exists elsewhere. Here the truth is no longer within, an actual order to be illuminated, but a virtual order to be created, fictionalized, in a medium unmistakably alien to the material it pictures. The first of these images suggests a metaphysical ontology of truth, the second a rhetoric of figuration which obviously can at best only approximate, only disfigure, the subject. It clearly marks its difference from that subject, and indeed is what it is because of that difference. We are back, in other words, to the two views of writing with which we began—as a direct rendering of the actual entities whose inner truths we must reveal, or as virtual points in a fictional matrix. The novel itself suggests ways of thinking through the relation between the two as diacritical conventions of the basic interpretive activity of culture.

The extent to which narrative practice in the novel shows interpretive interests at work on the "nonfiction" material can be seen in a number of ways that echo the previously cited work of Nance, De Bellis, and Tompkins on *In Cold Blood*. Jake, a detective and a friend of Capote's, is one narrator worth comment. He selects the case for the character "TC" as "something that he thought might interest" a novelist (p. 68), and he draws on his own literary tastes (Dickens, Trollope, Melville, and Twain are mentioned) to present matters to TC. One sees a number of instances of this literary framing of the event Jake literally reads from fiction to explain Quinn, he paces the timing of information for maximum effect, and he allows metaphor to introduce figurative displacement into a supposedly denotative case history in criminology (as when his chief is "jittery as a killer on Death Row," an interesting mixing of contraries). Perhaps he has no choice but to perceive events in terms of Dickens's search for hidden connections, people in terms of characters in nineteenth-century novels, referential "facts" in terms of metaphorical figures—nonfiction in terms of fiction.

As for the larger topic of TC's narrative practice, one's first observation is that he plays well the role of "narratee" for Jake. For example, when Jake tells him of the rattlesnake murders, TC plays the role of ideal reader, co-creating in his imagination the scene Jake outlines:

> But the sound of the wind was only a murmur in my head underneath the racket of rattling rattlesnakes, hissing tongues. I saw the car dark under a hot sun, the swirling serpents, the human heads growing green, expanding with poison. I listened to the wind, letting it wipe the scene away. (p. 70)

Besides being a prime example of Capote's skill at description, the passage shows TC's willingness to go beyond the factual to imagine how it has come to be. A fictional narrative line is projected back of the "facts" of corpses to explain them, a quite mythic origin posited that in its fictiveness reiterates the book's qualification of any naïve understanding of its method, or that of detection, interpretation, or nonfiction. It also, of course, shapes the responses of TC's own readers—of us, that is—as he does later when he marvels at the "mathematical element" in Clem Anderson's decapitation (p. 76), or when he underlines the suspense in Jake's tale of Addie ("You mean you're going to leave me hanging out here?" [p. 83]).

Lest we neglect our hermeneutic responsibilities, TC prods us from time to time by rendering facts as clues: "There were nine snakes. And nine members of the Blue River Committee. Nice quaint coincidence" (p. 97). By playing narratee so well, TC plots out within his novel the "real" readers' responses. In other words, those supposedly external to the narrative find themselves already anticipated there inside the text. One hears in the distance Roland Barthes collapsing the distinction between reader and text, but more conservatively, for the moment, we may note that TC exploits fully, as Capote's preface promises, the resources of fictional narratees in his nonfiction work.

TC exploits fictional narrators too, as it turns out. He paces his story as much like the omniscient novelist as Jake does; he finally remembers at one point of whom Quinn reminds him, but won't tell us until the time is ripe (p. 110). And he makes good use of Dickensian dreams; he speaks of

"Addie: her hair, tangled in watery undergrowths, drifted, in my dream, across her wavering drowned face like a bridal veil" (p. 127), anything but an innocent metaphor. An even more intense example of the classic dream device occurs earlier in the narrative:

> Oddly, sleep struck me as though I'd been hit by a thief's blackjack ... I entered some sphere between sleep and wake-fulness, my mind like a crystal lozenge, a suspended instrument that caught the reflections of spiraling images: a man's head among leaves, the windows of a car streaked with venom, the eyes of serpents sliding through heat-mist, fire flowing from the earth, scorched fists pounding at a cellar door, taut wire gleaming in the twilight, a torso on a roadway, a head among leaves, fire, fire, fire flowing like a river, river, river. Then a telephone rings. (p. 84)

At first glance this seems only a marvellously evocative passage that collects for the reader the various murders that have taken place. But the least bit of attention to its figures finds more of interest as well. The puzzle of reality, represented in the novel as crime, seems to have become pervasive, as TC cannot even nap without theft and assault giving shape to his sleep. Moreover, the "spheres" that normally exhaust the alternatives are here split by another, nameless sphere in which he finds himself.

Perhaps more interesting than the cosmology is what takes place there. His mind becomes "a crystal lozenge" that "caught the reflections" of the images he lists. The very materiality of his mental theater is an interesting anachronism for our age, but its epistemological implications may be even more so. That is, the lozenge is "crystal" or clear, and the images are "reflections" of something external to that mind, since crystals reflect particularly those images "spiraling" around the crystal. But if Jake has indeed not described, but TC imagined, the details, as we saw a moment ago, then these cannot be external images at all. And if they are made by TC, then he is hardly the neutral, objective, crystal clear window upon them, but rather the opaque colorist or producer of them. The superrealist, the nonfiction journalist reporting on "the way it was," might indeed aspire to the method of the crystal lozenge, but it seems oddly out of place here. Ah— one remembers, this is a dream, Capote only dreams of himself as the objective, nonfiction reporter. If nonfiction is thus the dream element of the narrative, that is to say of the fictional element, does that make the fictional element *more* real, deriving as it does from the flow of actual fictional narratives in culture? The interchange of contraries remains confusing, as in this passage when fire and water are equivalent. Fortunately for the analyst, "the telephone rings," giving us a line out of a literary device that absorbs pretensions to the non-literary, nonverbal, and nonfictional into its own dream structure.

What he finds "outside" the dream-set is not necessarily reassuring, however. Apparently casual allusions turn out to be not at all innocent. Early in the narrative, for example, while TC is watching Addie and Jake together, the allusions are to mannerists like Edith Wharton (p. 87) and Jane Austen (p. 94). By the time the mystery heats up, the allusions are to the likes of Eric Ambler (p. 105). After TC has left the scene for a while, another phone call takes him back—and, appropriately enough, it is Proust he reads (p. 120), the prime retrospective interpretive narrative that, as TC notes, is "rather like plunging into a tidal wave, destination unknown" (p. 120). The catastrophic imagery is justified, since Addie's life is swept away and, consistent with the imagery, by drowning. In other words, apparently inert allusions, always "justified" by the "realistic" context that cues them, are in fact a narrative line of literary frames that provide the appropriate sort of context within which to see these events taking place. To see them take place in such a context is not only to see them already interpreted in accordance with those frames, but to have one's responses plotted within the narrative by an all-but-omniscient narrator who exploits his knowledge of the materials, placing our responses in the sequence best suited to increasing their narrative impact upon us.

The imagery of the novel is no more crystalline in its treatment of fiction and nonfiction. In playing up the romance developing between Jake and Addie, a sort of sentimental subplot in this multiplotted novel, TC deploys some curious images. He says, for example, that "the style of the woman implied an erotic history complete with footnotes," a remarkably textual metaphor implying that either TC's perceptual framework or Addie's self-creation—or both—complies with specific narrative conventions. In the next sentence TC says that "the tension between them was as taut as the steel wire that had severed Clem Anderson's head" (pp. 86–87), a grotesque image conflating the desires of murder and sex, and prophetic of the consequences of the relationship fatal to both, though to Jake only metaphorically. Both metaphors invade reportage of objective facts with the interpretive figures of fiction.

The extent to which a mode of understanding preconstructs observation shows in passages like that in which TC notices Jake blowing smoke rings and decides that "the empty oval, floating through the air, seemed to carry with it an erotic message" (p. 89). Perhaps as another type of crystal lozenge this "empty oval" may be filled with whatever plot the narrator constructs, but it is clearly less a transparent window or neutral reflection than a flamboyant splash of rhetorical color upon the page. It is as heavy-handed as TC's parenthetical break away from Jake's vow to protect Addie to a scene he dreams up of wintry clumps of grass and "two spotted calves huddled side by side, lending each other comfort, protection: like Jake, like Addie" (pp. 107–8). Knowing when winter calves are sent to slaughter strengthens the reader's expectations that, come summer, Addie must die: after all, we have learned as well as Jake from Dickens and Trollope that plot resolutions conform to the miniature narrative epitomized in foregrounded imagery. It appears that when Capote combines the denotative language of journalism with the figurative language of fiction, he (inadvertently?) ends up clarifying how figures work in any discourse to betray the interpretive plots that writers-as-narrators impose upon whatever type of experience they set out to inscribe within their respective discursive orders. Baldly put, language as figure points to discourse as fiction.

To turn to the substance of TC's relation to the mystery late in the novel is to see how such confusions come to fruition. Good novel reader that he is, TC keeps looking for the univocal "key" to Quinn-as-character, finding it finally—or perhaps constructing it finally—by identifying him with a character in his own private psychodrama, the traumatically austere Reverend Snow. Perhaps it is worth pointing out that snow is another crystal lozenge allowing the narrative projectionist full freedom. On the basis of this identification, TC finds Quinn guilty, seeing him as a sufficiently self-righteous monomaniac to perpetrate the crimes. He even constructs the scenario for us; he is again not quite sleeping, and tells us that "Images formed, faded; it was as though I were mentally editing a motion picture" (p. 129). We might take him to be simply an earnest editor of images that form themselves or are otherwise external if we had not already been disabused of such a naïve sense of the narrative act. What we are in fact doing is watching TC fit the images *he* has imagined to the criteria for causal coherence, character consistency, and the like that he inherits from the genre of film and, by extension, from the history of philosophical assumptions presupposed by that genre.

For a full page, TC elaborates his feature-length dream of the way it was, but then after daybreak had "lessened my enthusiasm for fevered fantasizing," concludes that "unless Jake had evolved a theory more convincing than my own imagination had managed, then I preferred to forget it; I was satisfied to fall asleep remembering the coroner's common-sense verdict: *Accidental death by drowning*" (p. 130). Having followed through the dream version Jake cues him to, TC finds it wavering in the illumination of daybreak, the light of common sense—that journalistic look at just the facts that presumably dispenses with imaginative reconstruction. A few pages later, however, he is angry to discover that his "fevered fantasizing" "*is* Jake's story," according to a colleague of Jake's, "give or take a lotta little details" (p. 132). TC is "angry at him [Jake] for not having produced a solid solution, crestfallen that his conjectures were no better than mine." Strangely enough, the narratives constructed by detective and novelist coincide, the plot lines of nonfiction and fiction cross. Movie editor, novelist, reporter, sleuth, metalinguistic hermeneutic theorist—they are all the same, it would seem.

The novel presses even further, however, in the way in which it subtly allies and even confounds the discourse of interpretive narrative with those of madness and religion. The figure of madness appears in a number of forms, some of them quite bizarre. Mrs. Parsons, for example, is a morphine addict whom Jake describes as "a woman who has already left life. She's looking back through a door—without regret" (p. 78). But she is nonetheless important to Jake because on first seeing the little coffin her husband receives, and without knowing of its presence in the other cases, she feels "a shadow" fall across their lives, and knows he has been murdered despite the lack of any evidence to that effect. That is, although a morphine-crazed recluse, she duplicates Jake's reasoning and conclusion.

This connection might seem far-fetched were there not other and closer ties established between the writer/detective and the madman. Juanita Quinn is another strange case with hair "too black to be true," a "narrow skull" with a face "like a fist" featuring "bored onyx eyes" (p. 112). More strange than her appearance is her drugged behavior; she sits regally in a chair that "may well have once decorated the throne room of an Iberian castle" (p. 111), with a shivering Chihuahua and a guitar on her lap, watching a TV game show with the volume turned down: she is difficult to distract. But her case gets more curious when she explains herself to TC:

> You asked why I have the sound off. The only time I have the sound on is to hear the weather report. Otherwise, I just watch and imagine what's being said. If I actually listen, it puts me right to sleep. But just imagining keeps me awake. And I have to stay awake—at least till midnight. Otherwise, I'd never get any sleep at all. Where do you live? (p. 113)

She, like TC, struggles in a confusing zone between sleeping and waking, she too has her trials with the night, and she too busies herself "imagining" plots in order to keep the demons at bay.

If we look at TC himself, we find not only these general parallels to Juanita's patterns, but passages like this one that more specifically ally him to the figure of madness:

> Anxiety, as any expensive psychiatrist will tell you, is caused by depression; but depression, as the same psychiatrist will inform you on a second visit and for an additional fee, is caused by anxiety. I rotated around in that humdrum circle all afternoon. By nightfall the two demons had combined; while anxiety copulated with depression, I sat staring at Mr. Bell's controversial invention, fearing the moment when I would have to dial the Prairie Motel and hear Jake admit that the Bureau was taking him off the case. (p. 133)

As it turns out, his plot no more fits the silent technology he stares at than Juanita's—Jake is not off the case, at least not yet. But in following the pattern he shares with Juanita of giving voice to the silent machine, a pattern peculiarly appropriate to the writer, he enacts the epistemological model in which one "explains" a silent truth supposedly within the material, voicing the presence of what had been only partly apparent before. But he also enacts the recurrent confusion of that model when its verbal account turns out to differ from the merely visible, nonverbal order we call "facts." He attempts, in other words, to reflect like a crystal lozenge though in fact he is painting like an ardent colorist. Moreover, he is doing all this within the context of neurosis, the low level rage of anxiety and its quiet intransigence as depression, each of which are to be "explained" by the other in a typically circular hermeneutic. It is only in these strange fringe states that he can give form to the material, it would seem, but the form derives not from within the material or even necessarily within him, but from the cultural imagination, which transpires in a mental space outlawed by the categorizing order of reason.

Perhaps Capote is simply being inconsistent in repeatedly conflating such contraries, but perhaps also the text demonstrates that the difference between them is illusory, a rhetorical strategy to make way for creativity. In keeping with this recurrent theme, the novel also places religion within the same philosophical template. Jake seems almost serious in attributing his continuation on the case to an answered prayer (p. 82), suggesting that a hermeneutic of prayer (the "help me?" answered by Addie) is at times an essential detail within the detective's picture. TC adds another analogical element to the religious and the detective hermeneutics when he, as writer, makes use of the connection between Quinn and the Reverend Snow to decide upon his characterization of Quinn. Dragged as a boy into the river during a revival, TC tells us that

> I shut my eyes; I smelled the Jesus hair, felt the Reverend's arms carrying me downward into drowning blackness, then hours later lifting me into sunlight. My eyes, opening, looked into his grey, manic eyes. His face, broad but gaunt, moved closer, and he kissed my lips. I heard a loud laugh, an eruption like gunfire: "Checkmate!" (p. 118)

The passage is like a Church Homecoming for our critical themes: blackness and sunlight as the two extremes, the strange grey zone where stable qualities like time become distorted, the fusion of the religious order and the "manic" rage, the identification of preacher and (presumed) murderer, the seepage of raging metaphoric gunfire into a "friendly" game of chess. The transubstantiation of Jesus, Reverend Snow, and Quinn is an example of a basic movement of logocentric logic, the however temporary effacement of difference in order to produce identity out of mere similarity, just as TC here effaces the distinctions among the three and transfers from Snow to Quinn the messianic ego. The point is not whether the process achieves a working insight, but that figurative displacement is its basis.

This would seem, however, to produce a problem for us. Up to this point we have been undoing the false dichotomy of fiction and nonfiction, created as a space-making strategy by which they can take place, and can take the place of the unnamable, dreamlike, inconsistently imaged state wherein they seem to originate. Now, it seems, there is a simultaneous countermovement in which the culture is accused of assimilating different entities into (deceptive) identities. How does one explain this? Perhaps by first seeing that it is not an isolated occurrence, that Capote apparently felt it an important enough gesture to repeat it, and in fact to let it stand as the end of his multiple hermeneutic venture—as sleuth, as novelist, as nonfiction chronicler, and as personally involved inquirer.

In a last, powerful scene, TC goes back to the Blue River after Addie's death and Jake's departure from the case. Drawn to Quinn as the center of the question—the party he must imagine guilty without knowing for sure— TC comes to him, appropriately enough, while Quinn is wading in the river itself. Quinn laments that Jake had too many suspicions for them to have become friends, and that

> "he even thought I drowned poor Addie Mason!" He laughed; then scowled. "The way I look at it is: it was the hand of God." He raised his own hand, and the river, viewed between his spread fingers, seemed to weave between them like a dark ribbon. "God's work. His will." (p. 147)

He invokes the novel's version of the hermeneutic issue (whodunit?), and then in a manner more straightforward than that of other figures of the novel, makes explicit that what follows is *not* the way it is, but the "way I look at it." A narrator who affirms that his product is a fictive framework, a commentator upon nonfictional "realities," a monomaniac assuming cosmic knowledge, a possible murderer who may have chosen to appear before TC in the rubber suit that would provide the missing "how?" to TC's account of a death in those same waters, a religious believer who assigns causality to providence, Quinn here subsumes all the roles distributed throughout the novel to others. He becomes, were this one of Propp's folktales, all roles and functions. He even embodies in one sense the voice of TC, the actual narrator, for the river is a "dark ribbon," dark with the sinister themes of mass murder and hyperrational madness, and is figuratively woven as an implement in *his* fingers. It is a type of the writer's pen leaking its black flow of ink, and the final words of TC's narrative are the Answer Quinn proposes. It is an appropriately theological answer: God's work, the Word embodied in fact.

A madman utters the culture's central, commanding image for order: all cases, all differences, resolve themselves in the Word. Does it then require madness of a kind to affirm and maintain such an order, the order assumed by the kind of hermeneutic search that is reflected in this novel from the central cultural tradition? One notes the steady increase in TC's depressive anxieties and Jake's mania for evidence, ever more intense the longer circumstances resist reduction to the univocal question their inquiry poses; one begins as a result to doubt their binary logic of madness and order, guilt and innocence, fiction and nonfiction, figure and fact. Quinn thus becomes a figure that threatens the very ground rules of the project's nonfiction dimension, for he handles the ancillary discourses as all the same kind of (fictional) ordering, and collapses them into a self-mystifying narrative delusion.

Hence one must turn back to the text itself, to the preface to the text, and recognize the implications for our thinking about literary genres. What Capote set out to do was to discover the *"really* true," and he set out with the classic logocentric dichotomies of fiction and nonfiction—that is to say, figurative and literal or referential language—with its attendant tools of inside-outside divisions and the hierarchical rankings of the two. Capote seems to have sought to bring the reality outside fiction into its inside, and thus make it more real; or, alternatively, he wanted to bring the fiction outside reality into the nonfiction, to increase its "energy and esthetic excitements," as he put it in the preface. As these dichotomies fold in on one another, we discover not the naïve realist's belief that fiction is adequate to reality, but the contrary, that nonfiction is never adequate to reality, that its distinction from fiction is one of the primary deceptive maneuvers of logocentric logic by which it hypothesizes the space in which it transpires. The "nonfiction novel" is thus a tautology, not an oxymoron.

Moreover, by talking of the *"really* true," Capote seems to have raised again the notion that truth is the indwelling meaning of events or entities themselves, and that the nonfictional discourses to which he resorts will give him privileged access: logical deduction solves the hermeneutic crisis. What we find, in fact, is a great deal of disorientation on TC's part as he tries to carry out this program. We see him deploying all manner of interpretive frames—both the fictional devices of allusion, figurative language, generic conventions, and the nonfictional devices of the assumptions implicit in these ancillary discourses. The "really true" inheres in the discursive order of intelligibility. It is outside the events, in the narrative covering them with the writer's colors, not in them; or, alternatively, it is not inside the "faithful" narrative version of events, but outside that order in the assumptions implicit in the language and the discursive conventions from which and by which and in which that narrative is cast. Either way, Capote's "invention" of the nonfiction novel is both hoax and ingenious gathering of the full cultural resources into the act of narration, even if those resources have always been in fiction, if in slightly different guises, just as the fictional has always been there in alternative cultural discourses.

When Capote tells us that, after his conceptual breakthrough, "I set myself center stage, and reconstructed" experiences in his writing (p. xviii), he goes back to the necessarily egoistic positing of the frameworks within which those experiences are seen to take place. It doesn't matter whether such fictions are generated by creating binary myths to divide—and conquer—reality, or by assimilating that multifarious reality into an all but monomaniacal logocentric ego. The point in either case, as a tactitian might put it, is to deploy your forces so that things begin happening.

Notes

1. *The Worlds of Truman Capote* (New York: Stein and Day, 1970), pp. 184, 178. Most commentaries on the novel follow Nance's lead, perhaps most explicitly John Hollowell in his *Fact & Fiction: The New Journalism and the Nonfiction Novel* (Chapel Hill: Univ. of North Carolina Press, 1977). Hollowell quotes Nance and Meyer Levin's definition of the "documentary novel" with approval. Jack De Bellis surveys some five thousand revisions Capote worked into the novel between its serialized and book forms, concluding that its factual accuracy is questionable and apparently subordinated to the subliminal goal of working out, novelistically, Capote's complex relationship to the South and to "the dual vision of his fiction" it gave him (p. 535), and he alludes to an earlier criticism of the novel's factual reliability by Phillip K. Tompkins in an article in *Esquire*. The De Bellis essay is "Visions and Revisions: Truman Capote's *In Cold Blood*," *Journal of Modern Literature*, 7 (1979), 519–36. Helen S. Garson talks of the way the novel is "mingling realism with novelistic imagination" (p. 143), an opposition that shows how completely within the fictional field she considers the type (in *Truman Capote* [New York: Frederick Ungar, 1980]). Kenneth T. Reed shows anxiety closer to the surface in emphasizing the "reordering and proportioning" of the orchestration but in seeing also no "distortion of fact" (in *Truman Capote* [Boston: Twayne Publishers, 1981], p. 112). See too Ronald Weber's *The Literature of Fact: Literary Nonfiction in American Writing* (Athens: Ohio Univ. Press, 1980); Weber admires the extent to which Capote draws us "into a world of meaning and inner coherence" (p. 73), "while remaining strictly within the historical record" (p. 80), a judgment perhaps too indulgent.

2. Mas'ud Zavarzadeh, *The Mythopoeic Reality: The Postwar American Nonfiction Novel* (Urbana: Univ. of Illinois Press, 1976), p. 68.

3. Alfred Kazin, in *Bright Book of Life: American Novelists and Storytellers from Hemingway to Mailer* (Notre Dame: Univ. of Notre Dame Press, 1980 [1973]), makes the same shift from quite a different perspective, summing up *In Cold Blood* as "a 'novel' in the form of fact" (p. 210) Both writers, in other words, feel the need for quotation marks around the same half of the nonfiction novel. Kazin, however, is more what Zavarzadeh would call a "liberal-humanist," with his concern for the tension between "our participation in the story [being] more narrow and helpless than [in] a real novel" (p. 218) and the books aim "to give us this mental control over the frightening example of what is most uncontrolled in human nature" (p. 216). The trouble with the genre for Kazin is that the preoccupation with senseless

crime "relieves the liberal imagination of responsibility and keeps it a spectator" (p. 219) of reality, rather than achieving what Zavarzadeh disparages as the "totalizing" goals of "liberal-humanist" fiction.

4. Zavarzadeh, p. 68.

5. Perhaps a work like Derrida's *Writing and Difference* (trans. Alan Bass [Chicago: Univ. of Chicago Press, 1978]) is the most notorious demonstration of a basic cultural myth he calls "logocentrism" in a whole galaxy of discourses including mysticism, sociology, psychology, linguistics, anthropology, and so forth. But see also Wilson Snipes, "The Biographer as a Center of Reference," *biography* 5, No. 3 (1982), 215–25, for a study of that nonfictional genre as a version of the way relativity figures in history as well as in physics. One may think also of Thomas Kuhn's *The Structure of Scientific Revolutions* (2nd ed. [Chicago: Univ. of Chicago Press, 1970]) as a study of a kind of cultural fiction he calls "paradigms," imaginative orderings of the universe which shape even science, that bastion of supposedly objective nonfiction.

6. John Hellmann comes closer to this position than any commentator I know, in *Fables of Fact: The New Journalism as New Fiction* (Urbana: Univ. of Illinois Press, 1981). He argues the distinction between new journalism (and the nonfiction novel) and other forms of fiction as that between the contracts they establish with the reader: the latter "points outward toward the actual world without ever deviating from observations of that world except in forms—such as authorial speculation or fantasy—which are immediately obvious as such to the reader" (p. 27). As in all fiction, the focus is upon "a microcosmic selection, shaping, and interpretation of events of the macrocosm into a text, a construct representing not events, but an individual consciousness's experience of them" (pp. 25–26). Hellmann is acutely alert to the illusoriness of any direct, unmediated perception of actual events, pointing out that even an historical character like Hubert Humphrey "that the reader knows outside his experience of a text is an interpretively selected and ordered construct of impressions, as is the author's, whether arrived at through first-hand knowledge or (more typically) already interpreted as received from the mass media" (p. 31). But Hellmann is probably more inclined than I to accept that there is something called "external facts" with which a writer can begin. In actual practice, such "facts" are inevitably textual episodes from the moment they form in one's consciousness.

7. The quotations from the preface and the novel come from the paperback edition (New York: New American Library, 1981) and are noted parenthetically.

BRUCE BAWER

Capote's Children

Truman Capote, who died last summer at the age of fifty-eight, was one of a handful of American novelists who became famous at a very early age in the years following the Second World War. Perhaps the three most celebrated of these writers were Gore Vidal (whose *Williwaw* appeared in 1946, when he was nineteen), Norman Mailer (whose *The Naked and the Dead* was issued two years later, when he was twenty-five), and Capote (who published *Other Voices, Other Rooms* in 1949, at the age of twenty-three). If Mailer and Vidal spent the early part of their careers climbing out of derivative ruts and attempting to find their own voices, Capote was an original from the start. This is not to suggest that he did not, in the manner of every young writer, learn from his antecedents. *Other Rooms, Other Voices* is riddled with Southern Gothic touches—grotesque characters, haunting scenes—that are reminiscent of Faulkner and Carson McCullers; its lyrical style and elegiac tone (a tone that was to stay with Capote forever, however radically his style might change) recall Willa Cather; and the situation and the contours of the plot bring to mind both *Jane Eyre* and *The Turn of the Screw*. For all this, to read *Other Voices, Other Rooms* is not to catalogue influences but to appreciate the way Capote makes these varied borrowings over into something entirely his own.

From *The New Criterion* 3, no. 10 (June 1985). © 1985 by The Foundation for Cultural Review, Inc.

Other Voices, Other Rooms charts the path toward self-discovery of an intelligent, rather delicate thirteen-year-old, Joel Knox, who, as the novel opens, is finding his way to the grand, dilapidated back-country home of his invalid father, Mr. Sansom, and his stepmother, Miss Amy, neither of whom he has ever met. Joel has been sent for by these two, but, as he eventually discovers, the summons was really the work of the third member of the household: his odd cousin Randolph, who appears one day, ghost-like and dressed as a woman, at an upstairs window. Randolph's yen for Joel is obvious, and at the end of the novel Joel recognizes that his own fate is, to put it delicately, bound up with Randolph's:

> His mind was absolutely clear. He was like a camera waiting for its subject to enter focus. The wall yellowed in the meticulous setting of the October sun, and the windows were rippling mirrors of cold, seasonal color. Beyond one, someone was watching him. All of him was dumb except his eyes. They knew. And it was Randolph's window. Gradually the blinding sunset drained from the glass, darkened, and it was as if snow were falling there, flakes shaping snow-eyes, hair: a face trembled like a white beautiful moth, smiled. She beckoned to him, shining and silver, and he knew he must go: unafraid, not hesitating, he paused only at the garden's edge where, as though he'd forgotten something, he stopped and looked back at the bloomless, descending blue, at the boy he had left behind.

Capote never stopped looking back at that boy. The innocence of childhood, the tragedy of having to trade it in for the sordidness and disillusionment of adulthood: these themes haunt all of Capote's major works. The heroes of his novels are invariably sensitive souls, aliens in the world of civilized, responsible adults, who are tortured by their inability to let go of childhood.

Critics have leveled many complaints against *Other Voices, Other Rooms*: that it hasn't got much of a plot, that it doesn't add up to anything, that it's intellectually barren. It's a mood piece, they complain, a stylistic tour de force. Perhaps. But what a mood, what a style! One marvels at the assured prose, at this young writer's ability to sweep one up and carry one, without a misstep, through a mysterious landscape which is to the real Deep South as Hardy's Wessex is to Dorset. One marvels, too, at his ability to de-familiarize—without a trace of self-consciousness—that most tiredly familiar of all first-novel genres, the *Bildungsroman*.

For almost a decade after *Other Voices, Other Rooms*, Capote produced one largish project per year. 1949: *A Tree of Night* (a story collection). 1950: *Local Color* (travel essays). 1951: *The Grass Harp* (a novel). 1952: the stage adaptation (unsuccessful) of *The Grass Harp*. 1953: the film *Beat the Devil*. 1954: book and lyrics (including the jazz standard "A Sleepin' Bee") for a Broadway musical, *House of Flowers*, with music by Harold Arlen. 1956: *The Muses Are Heard*, a journal of Capote's trip to the Soviet Union with the cast of *Porgy and Bess*. Clearly, in the early Fifties Capote was already developing the fascination with those glitzy extra-literary milieus (showbiz, café society, the jet set) which were to usurp much of his time and energy over the ensuing years, and evincing a remarkable willingness (and ability) to apply his talents to a variety of genres. Despite this dazzling (and, perhaps, dismaying) versatility, however, Capote continued to devote himself, throughout the 1950s, primarily to prose fiction.

Like *Other Voices, Other Rooms*, *The Grass Harp*, his major work of the period, offers a setting in the Deep South, eccentric relatives, grotesque neighbors, an intelligent yet delicate boy's confrontation with adulthood, a thinly veiled homosexual theme—and rich, romantic prose:

> When was it that I first heard of the grass harp? Long before the autumn we lived in the China tree; an earlier autumn, then; and of course it was Dolly who told me, no one else would have known to call it that, a grass harp.
>
> If on leaving town you take the church road you soon will pass a glaring hill of bonewhite slabs and brown burnt flowers: this is the Baptist cemetery.... Below the hill grows a field of high Indian grass that changes color with the seasons: go to see it in the fall, late September, when it has gone red as sunset, when scarlet shadows like firelight breeze over it and the autumn winds strum on its dry leaves sighing human music, a harp of voices.
>
> Beyond the field begins the darkness of River Woods. It must have been one of those September days when we were there in the woods gathering roots that Dolly said: Do you hear? that is the grass harp, always telling a story—it knows the stories of all the people on the hill, of all the people who ever lived, and when we are dead it will tell ours, too.

The speaker here is sixteen-year-old Collin, who lives in a small town with his father's cousins Verena (a tyrant) and the above-mentioned Dolly (the first of many endearing child-women in Capote's work). When Verena

returns from a trip to Chicago with a vulgar man named Morris Ritz, who
insists upon learning the formula for Dolly's secret herbal medicine—he and
Verena want to patent it, market it, and reap the rewards—Collin, Dolly, and
their black friend Catherine escape to a tree house in the woods.
Complications ensue—some forced and farcical, some melodramatic: the
town descends upon them, threatening legal action and physical harm; the
local judge and Riley, the town hellion (and Collin's idol), join them in the
tree; Ritz absconds with Verena's money; Collin and his companions
abandon the tree house; Dolly dies of a stroke; Riley marries; Collin packs
his bags and leaves town, "not foresee[ing] that I would travel the road and
dream the tree until they had drawn me back." *The Grass Harp* demonstrates
that Capote's aims had changed somewhat since his first book: he wanted to
be not only moving but *funny*, to create a mood *and* tell a relatively involved
story, and to concentrate less on his boy-hero and more on the people around
him. But the style of this short novel did not, for the most part, depart
markedly from the lyrical, meditative manner of *Other Voices, Other Rooms*.

Capote continued to develop, though, and in the same direction. By
the time of *Breakfast at Tiffany's* (1958), he was even more concerned with
developing a plot, being humorous, and looking beyond his protagonist (who
had, by now, grown into a young man); and he had, fortunately, developed a
style that suited these ends perfectly. That style, *New Yorker*ishly terse and
precise, is reminiscent of J. D. Salinger, and so is the setting, "a brownstone
in the East Seventies ... during the early years of the war." The hero of the
novella is a fledgling Southern (and, though he never says so explicitly,
homosexual) writer who lives in that brownstone; the heroine, Holly
Golightly, is a gorgeous, stylish playgirl in the apartment directly below, who
peppers her conversation with French expressions, earns her living by dating
middle-aged men and delivering coded messages to a "sweet" Mafia kingpin
named Sally Tomato, and hopes to marry very, very rich. *Breakfast at Tiffany's*
marks a switch in Capote's stylistic emphasis from evocative description to
dialogue—which is, in its own way, equally evocative:

> "Be a darling, darling, rub some oil on my back." While I was
> performing this service, she said: "O. J. Berman's in town, and
> listen, I gave him your story in the magazine. He was quite
> impressed. He thinks maybe you're worth helping. But he says
> you're on the wrong track. Negroes and children: who cares?"
> "Not Mr. Berman, I gather."
> "Well, I agree with him. I read that story twice. Brats and
> niggers. Trembling leaves. *Description*. It doesn't *mean* anything."

The twist in *Breakfast at Tiffany's* is that Holly (who seems here, perhaps, to have been reading something very much like *The Grass Harp*) is a hillbilly girl, real name Lulamae, the runaway wife of a horse doctor in Tulip, Texas, who is old enough to be her grandfather. She is, at bottom, a scared, vulnerable Southern child, a self-exile, compelled by her helpless fear of the responsibilities of adulthood to wander far from home, binding herself to no one, trying desperately to lose sight of her terror and loneliness among the bright lights and the nightclub crowds of New York.

The more closely one looks at *Breakfast at Tiffany's* the more difficult it is to avoid feeling that the novella is something of a schizophrenic act on Capote's part. One side of him (the disciplined, mature writer) observes the other (the wild, frivolous party-goer, enthralled by criminals and enamored of the very, very rich, who refuses to grow up). The ego lives upstairs, the id downstairs. Not that this Freudian schema is at all conspicuous; on the contrary, few contemporary American novels provide as good an example as *Breakfast at Tiffany's* does of Flaubertian economy, elegance, and (seeming) objectivity. It is Capote's finest work—witty, affecting, not a word wasted.

Many, of course, would accord that distinction to *In Cold Blood* (1966). This study of the 1958 murder of the Clutter family of Holcomb, Kansas, is undeniably riveting, but Capote's lifelong tendency to identify with the outsider led him, in this instance, to present the facts in such a way that the reader has to struggle to avoid sympathizing with the murderers, Perry Smith and Richard Hickock. As Capote describes them, the Clutters are *Reader's Digest*-reading robots, fudge-baking clones, church-going zombies, who have no great ambitions, no profound torments, no interest in pursuing anything other than the unexamined life. Contrasted with these card-carrying members of the Bible Belt *booboisie* are the two killers. The Clutters' murderers—Perry Smith especially—fascinated Capote. In Perry, a small, childlike man with an I.Q. of 130, a carful of books, maps, poems, and letters, and a preoccupation with his memories of boyhood, Capote appears to have seen a sensitive soul—and, one suspects, yet another alter ego. Though the tone of *In Cold Blood* is controlled and impersonal, the fact is that Capote developed a warm friendship with the murderers during his years of research; at the end, he accompanied them to the scaffold, wept for days over their deaths, and even paid for their grave markers. One wishes, for the sake of *In Cold Blood*, that he had been as close to the Clutters. Even that, though, would probably not have been enough: Capote's fascination with murder and murderers (which by no means ended with *In Cold Blood*) was too profound, and his aloofness from moral considerations (in these matters, at least) too extreme, to allow for much authorial sympathy for the victims.[1]

Capote trumpeted that he had, in *In Cold Blood*, created a new literary form, the "non-fiction novel." Some critics hailed this "invention," others dismissed it. Norman Mailer suggested that Capote's swing to nonfiction bespoke "a failure of imagination," and then (as Capote spent the next eighteen years pointing out) wrote *The Armies of the Night*, a "novel-as-history," and won the Pulitzer Prize for it. *In Cold Blood* is, of course, no novel; but it is a very sophisticated piece of New Journalism, the sort of handsomely written, subtly partisan reportage that only a gifted author of fiction could have concocted.

After *In Cold Blood*, Capote continued to experiment with genre. He published less and less; during most of the nearly two decades between the publication of *In Cold Blood* and his death, Capote claimed to be working hard at a book called *Answered Prayers*, which he described as "a variation on the nonfiction novel." (The title "is a quote from Saint Thèrése, who said: 'More tears are shed over answered prayers than unanswered ones.'") Chapters from this work-in-progress appeared in *Esquire* during the mid-Seventies, and the information they disclosed about certain of Capote's café society friends—who, by that time, seemed to have become far more important to him than his writing—supposedly turned all of them against him. (This rejection, in turn, reportedly drove him to the heavy drinking and drug-taking that brought on his death.) The excerpts didn't do Capote's literary reputation much good either. Critics saw *Answered Prayers* as gossip, not serious literature—the work of a man grown lazy and self-indulgent. And they were, unfortunately, right: the *Esquire* excerpts represent a surrender, on Capote's part, to those more puerile tendencies that were evident in—but did not, at any rate, tyrannize—his earlier work. To be sure, one can discern, in reading the excerpts (which *are* beautifully composed), that Capote did have at least a ghost of a serious literary intention here. He wanted to say the usual things about fame, wealth, and the wages of ambition, while doing for the New York society of the 1970s what Edith Wharton had done for the New York society of the 1870s. The excerpts do succeed in one sense: they prove beyond a doubt that most of the rich ladies who spend their afternoons at La Côte Basque and La Grenouille are dull and shallow. This, indeed, seems to be Capote's main point. But why, if these women *are* so dull and shallow, would anyone want to spend a decade of his life reproducing their silly chatter and collecting their gossip—or, for that matter, keeping them company? It is, to be sure, possible that *Answered Prayers*, as Capote envisioned it, would have added up to a profound, penetrating novel of contemporary manners. But the published excerpts, as they stand, do not penetrate very deeply.[2]

It appears likely that we shall never know precisely what *Answered Prayers* could have been. An article by Julie Baumgold which appeared last fall in *New York* magazine told the story. After Capote's death, his biographer, his editor, and his lawyer searched his Long Island house but failed to find a single page of the manuscript that he had claimed, for so many years, to be toiling over, and which (though he had never shown it to anybody) he had expostulated upon at length in countless interviews. After looking everywhere, Capote's friends faced what appeared to be the unpleasant truth: there was no *Answered Prayers*; Capote had seemingly been lying for years about his progress on it. It is, of course, possible that he had produced hundreds of pages of his intended *magnum opus*, but had found them unworthy and destroyed them in the course of attempted revision.

In the preface to his final book, *Music for Chamclcons*. Capote indicated that he had stopped work on *Answered Prayers* as the result of "a creative crisis and a personal one" that came upon him at the same time. These crises, as it turned out, "altered my entire comprehension of writing, my attitude toward art and life and the balance between the two, and my understanding of the difference between what is true and what is *really* true." The upshot is that he began to rewrite *Answered Prayers* in an entirely new style. That style—which dominates *Music for Chameleons*—represents yet another step in the direction Capote had been moving all along: toward greater concision and "realism," a heavier reliance upon dialogue, and a more comprehensive combination of forms. The idea was to "combine within a single form ... all [he knew] about every other form of writing.... A writer ought to have all his colors, all his abilities available on the same palette for mingling (and, in suitable instances, simultaneous application)."

The longest and most effective of the pieces in *Music for Chameleons*, a "nonfiction short novel" called "Handcarved Coffins," describes a bizarre-but-true series of crimes that Capote followed closely during the late Seventies; the new style works well here, and the story, though shorn of the depth and detail of *In Cold Blood*, has an immediacy, an emotional force, and a quality of genuine suspensefulness and terror that Capote had never achieved before. The "Conversational Portraits" that occupy nearly half of *Music for Chameleons* are somewhat less ambitious. As the collective title indicates, each of these short pieces consists of the record of a conversation between Capote and someone he finds interesting—Pearl Bailey, Bobby Beausoleil (of Manson Family fame), Mary Sanchez (Capote's cleaning lady). In the most celebrated of these pieces, "A Beautiful Child," Capote describes his cavortings on an April day in 1955 in Manhattan with Marilyn Monroe, whom he sees as a Holly Golightly-like child-woman, a beautiful innocent adrift on the corrupt seas of life. The cavortings end at twilight on South Street Seaport:

> MARILYN: Remember, I said if anybody ever asked you what I was like, what Marilyn Monroe was *really* like—well, how would you answer them? (Her tone was teaseful, mocking, yet earnest, too: she wanted an honest reply) I bet you'd tell them I was a slob. A banana split.
> TC: Of course. But I'd also say ...
> (The light was leaving. She seemed to fade with it, blend with the sky and clouds, recede beyond them. I wanted to lift my voice louder than the seagulls' cries and call her back: Marilyn! Marilyn, why did everything have to turn out the way it did? Why does life have to be so fucking rotten?)
> TC: I'd say ...
> MARILYN: I can't hear you.
> TC: I'd say you are a beautiful child.

There is some lovely writing in the work that Capote published after *In Cold Blood*, and the mixed-salad style of *Music for Chameleons* is often surprisingly successful. But—as pieces like "A Beautiful Child" graphically illustrate—the appeal of much of this work has relatively little to do with its literary merits. Capote, in his zeal to write "nonfiction novels" and "nonfiction short stories," may well have thought that he was being faithful to "what is *really* true," but all he was doing, in actuality, was neglecting his obligation as a literary artist to create, to order, and thereby to serve not merely personal and superficial truths but universal ones. It is an obligation to which Capote was attentive for so long, and which he fulfilled with such distinction, that his ultimate renunciation of it (manifestly well-intentioned though it may have been) is particularly disheartening. Because of this renunciation—and for the other reasons I have suggested—it is, perhaps, easier to celebrate the fine literary talent Capote was gifted with than to applaud many of the uses he made of it. The Capote-like narrator of one of the published *Answered Prayers* excerpts, writer P. B. Jones, remarks at one point: "I knew I was a bastard but forgave myself because I was *born* a bastard—a talented one whose sole obligation was to his talent." This sounds exactly like Capote talking about himself, and it describes what may well have been Capote's tragic flaw: that throughout most of his adult life, he considered himself to be responsible only to his talent. It seems never to have occurred to him that his talent, in turn, might have its own responsibilities.

NOTES

1. In *Conversations with Capote*, published last year, Lawrence Grobel asks: "Have you ever wondered why you are able to relate so well to murderers?" Capote replies: "Because right away they realized that I wasn't passing any judgment on them. I had no opinion about them as a person regarding the fact that they'd killed...." The book—which consists mostly of insulting remarks about nearly everyone Capote ever knew—was published by the New American Library (244 pages, $14.95). Also recently issued is *Three by Truman Capote*, which includes *Other Voices, Other Rooms; Breakfast at Tiffany's*; and *Music for Chameleons* (Random House, 358 pages, $12.95).

2. Interestingly, as far back as 1964, Norman Mailer had foreseen both *Answered Prayers* and its consequences. In his famous *Esquire* piece, "Quick and Expensive Comments on the Talent in the Room," Mailer wrote of Capote: "I would suspect he hesitates between the attractions of Society which enjoys and so repays him for his unique gifts, and the novel he could write of the gossip column's real life, a major work, but it would banish him forever from his favorite world."

BLAKE ALLMENDINGER

The Room Was Locked, with the Key on the Inside:
Female Influence in Truman Capote's
"My Side of the Matter"

> Grobel: "Has any American writer had an influence
> on you as a writer?"
> Capote: "No American writer has."
> —*Conversations with Capote*

I

The apartment was in the wildest disorder—the furniture broken
and thrown about in all directions. There was only one bedstead;
and from this the bed had been removed, and thrown into the
middle of the floor. On a chair lay a razor, besmeared with blood.
On the hearth were two or three long and thick tresses of gray
human hair, also dabbled with blood, and seeming to have been
pulled out by the roots.[1]

So Poe describes the scene of the crime, in "The Murders in the Rue
Morgue." He startles the reader with a graphic depiction of the bedroom,
but he stumps the reader with a detail that has since become a staple of
detective fiction. Auguste Dupin learns, on forcing the door, that

From *Studies in Short Fiction* 24, no. 3 (Summer 1987). © 1987 by Studies in Short Fiction.

no person was seen. The windows, both of the back and front
room, were down and firmly fastened from within.... The door
leading from the front room into the passage was locked, with the
key on the inside.[2]

Dupin wrestles with the right of access to a locked room. In a similar fashion,
critics struggle with the seductive image and mythic biography of Truman
Capote. In conversations, interviews, and the preface to his last book, *Music
for Chameleons*, Capote denies the influence of other writers on his work.
Describing his own development, he conjures up the image of a locked
room—of a writer who withdraws from the influence of society, to create.
Critics have been less successful than Poe's detective in solving the puzzle of
the room, locked from within. In the last thirty years, they have accepted the
proclamations of a man whose conversation was often more convincing than
his prose; whose own texts contradict the denials of literary influence. Books
and articles have linked Capote to the work of his contemporaries in only a
vague, suggestive sense, but a piece from his early period draws specifically
upon Eudora Welty. "My Side of the Matter" is a clear reconstruction of her
short story, "Why I Live at the P.O.," and a case study in the anxiety of
female influence. In his response to Welty, Capote alters the gender of his
characters to depict a battle between the sexes and centers the plot on a male
protagonist, accused of stealing from a woman.

II

In the preface to *Music for Chameleons*, Capote says: "I started writing when
I was eight—out of the blue, uninspired by any example."[3] Capote means to
impress the reader with the emergence of his art, as a magician seeks to
startle the audience, pulling a rabbit out of his hat. Here and elsewhere,
Capote loads the denial of literary influence with a rhetorical force that seeks
to amaze the audience and suggest that writing is an uninspired feat. In
Conversations with Capote, the author belittles Ezra Pound by telling
Lawrence Grobel that the poet sought help from T.S. Eliot. He adds: "I've
never had anybody that I could show things to and ask their opinion."[4] He
insists that Norman Mailer and other contemporaries have drawn from his
work to produce the non-fiction novel and have won awards for their
unacknowledged debt to his own novel, *In Cold Blood*. But he denies that he,
in turn, has drawn from Henry Adams or Hemingway, as Malcolm Cowley
suggests.[5] He reiterates this statement throughout a series of interviews with
Grobel and insists upon it with an air of protestation.

> I don't think of myself in terms of relationships with other writers at all and I don't feel in competition with other writers. Because I don't write about the same things as any other writer that I know of does. Or have the same interests. Or as a personality that's in any kind of conflict with any other writer. I have absolutely no envy of any other writer.[6]

Capote suggests that literary influence is not a tradition, which bonds together writers in a helpful sense, but a psychological abnormality which brands the writer as psychotic with a "personality" disorder, in "conflict" or "competition" with tradition. Capote relates self-sufficiency to self-esteem and isolates himself from the canon.

In doing so, he builds an image around his own identity as an autonomous writer. He tells Grobel that he hid in his bedroom and started to write when he was eight years old. "I mean, really seriously, so seriously that I dared never mention it to anybody. I spent hours every day writing and never showed it to a teacher."[7] Capote allows the reader to imagine that he has fought off the curious and withdrawn from the world to write in his room. In the preface to *Music of Chameleons*, he says that his family sought to discover the purpose of his confinement. "Yet I never discussed my writing with anyone; if someone asked what I was up to all those hours, I told them I was doing my school homework."[8] Grobel accepts the scenario or finds the image of the locked room sufficiently interesting to include in a preface to his interview. He tells the reader that Capote was inspired to write *Other Voices, Other Rooms* during a winter walk in the forest. "When he finally reached home, he went straight to his room, locked the door, got into bed fully clothed, and ... wrote: '*Other Voices, Other Rooms*—a novel by Truman Capote!'"[9]

III

The image of the locked room seems to have satisfied critics for the last thirty years. *In Cold Blood* has drawn attention because of the connection between the non-fiction novel and its precursors: *The Education of Henry Adams* and Theodore Dreiser's *An American Tragedy*. But "My Side of the Matter" has been overshadowed by other stories in *A Tree of Night*. Since winning the O. Henry Awards, both "Miriam" and "Shut a Final Door" have received scrutiny, but articles dealing with these stories discuss themes and predicaments that attract most readers of Southern American fiction: the

Gothic, the grotesque, the obsession with the past, the use of local color and dialect. American critics have skirted the issue of influence since the publication of *A Tree of Night* and have focused on major stories in the collection.

"My Side of the Matter" borrows its plot from Welty's work, "Why I Live at the P.O." Both stories tell of a woman who returns home to her family, with child, and precipitates an argument that leads to the withdrawal of the narrator from other members of the household. Stella-Rondo returns with Shirley-T., a child she has "adopted."[10] Sister challenges the parenthood of Shirley-T., accuses Stella-Rondo of having borne the child herself, and provokes an argument which broadens in scope as it builds to climax. Systematically throughout the narrative, Papa-Daddy, Mama, Uncle Rondo and Shirley-T. turn against Sister and persuade her to leave the house. She moves to the post office.

> And if Stella-Rondo should come to me this minute, on bended knees, and *attempt* to explain the incidents of her life with Mr. Whitaker, I'd simply put my fingers in both my ears and refuse to listen. (56)

Marge returns to her aunts, three months pregnant, in "My Side of the Matter." Both Eunice and Olivia-Ann disparage her husband—the narrator—belittle his manhood, and question the fatherhood of the child. They antagonize Sylvester and succeed in turning his wife and their maid against him. After a skirmish, Marge's husband locks himself in the parlor, defies the other members of the family and, like Sister, determines to spite them.

> Oh, yes, they've started singing a song of a very different color. But as for me—I give them a tune on the piano every now and then just to let them know I'm cheerful.[11]

Capote characterizes the people in his story by exploiting particular elements that occur in Welty's earlier work. Uncle Rondo becomes ridiculous when he appears "in the hall in one of Stella-Rondo's flesh-colored kimonos, all cut on the bias, like something Mr. Whitaker probably thought was gorgeous" (48). Capote uses the same garment to undercut the authority of Eunice and to mock her romantic self-image. "She troops around the house, rain or shine, in this real old-fashioned nighty, calls it a kimono, but it isn't anything in this world but a dirty flannel nighty" (197). Olivia-Ann has a pathetic, romantic attachment to Gary Cooper and has "one trunk and two suitcases full of his photos" (200). Her fantasy has its counterpart in the trivial feud between Sister and Stella-Rondo, who fight over Mr. Whitaker while sitting for "Pose Yourself" photos (46). Papa-Daddy intimidates the community of China Grove, as well as his family, by exploiting his alleged wealth and power. He uses his position to procure the office of postmistress for Sister and to marshal the town against her when she leaves. "There are always people who will quit buying stamps just to get on the right side of Papa-Daddy" (56). Welty exploits the comedy by characterizing Papa-Daddy as a man who denies the rumors of wealth, but capitalizes on them to wield power. Sister says: "He's real rich. Mama says he is, he says he isn't" (47). Capote puts Eunice in the same position. "Not that she hasn't got plenty of money! Naturally she says she hasn't but I know she has ..." (197). Sylvester attributes the influence of Eunice to her status in Admiral's Mill.

> Of course anything Eunice says is an order from headquarters as not a breathing soul in Admiral's Mill can stand up and say he doesn't owe her money.... (197)

Capote caricatures the battle between David and Goliath by juxtaposing the status of Eunice with that of the narrator. While Eunice conceals her funds and denies her wealth, Sylvester exaggerates the importance of his job in Mobile, and consistently refers to his "perfectly swéll position clerking at the Cash'n'Carry" (196-197). Welty also pits the authority of Papa-Daddy against the subordinate Sister, who runs "the next to smallest P.O. in the entire state of Mississippi" (47).

Welty and Capote tell their stories in the first-person. In part, they do so to color the narrative with a silly urgency and impromptu exaggeration, both of which help to characterize the tall tale. Sister and Sylvester are obsessed with their own importance, the injustice of "life," and the righteous indignation which motivates their behavior. Their ramblings also enliven the events of the past, turning them into oral reconstructions of the immediate present. Run-on syntax, slang, idiomatic phrases, and italicized words animate experience and imitate the inflection of vocal speech patterns. Sister and Sylvester talk to their audience and recreate their scenes, using rhetoric to grab the attention or gain the sympathy of the reader. Sister uses one device which occurs nowhere else in the works of Welty: the recreation of speech tempos through the hyphenation of letters within a single word. She prepares the reader for the reaction of Papa-Daddy, who rebels against the notion that he should cut off his beard. Stella-Rondo says: "'Papa-Daddy,

Sister says she fails to understand why you don't cut off your beard.' So Papa-Daddy l-a-y-s down his knife and fork!" (47). The reader anticipates the response of Papa-Daddy, who slowly l-a-y-s down his utensils and prepares to put up his dukes. Capote appropriates the same device in a dialogue between Eunice and Marge. Marge describes the narrator as "the best-looking" man she knows, and the narrator says: "Eunice eyes me u-p and d-o-w-n and says, 'Tell him to turn around'" (198). Again, the elongation of the phrase "u-p and d-o-w-n" enables the reader to see Eunice, as she scans the body of the narrator with careful scrutiny, and prepares the reader for the sarcastic comment which follows the pause. "'You sure must've picked the runt of the litter. Why, this isn't any sort of man at all'" (198).

Two other strategies have their counterparts in "My Side of the Matter": the comic one-liner, used to describe a character, and the rhetorical question, addressed to the reader. Sister systematically slays her antagonist-of-the-moment with comic barbs throughout the story. "Papa-Daddy is about a million years old and's got this long-long beard" (47). "You ought to see Mama, she weighs two hundred pounds and has real tiny feet" (50). She exaggerates the age and weight of her family and undercuts one aspect of their appearance by insisting on the incongruity of another. Welty turns the longevity of Papa-Daddy into a joke and makes the grandfather into a caricature of Methuselah, with a "long-long beard." Sister's description of Mama cannot bear scrutiny, any more than her mother's "real tiny feet" can possibly bear the weight of her "two hundred pounds." Capote's description of Eunice bears more than a faint resemblance to Welty's description of Mama. "Eunice is this big old fat thing with a behind that must weigh a tenth of a ton" (197). Elsewhere, Olivia-Ann is "real pale and skinny and has a mustache" (197). Marge has "no looks, no body, and no brains whatsoever" (196). The narrator resents the interference of Eunice, Marge, and Olivia-Ann by telling Eunice about Mrs. Harry Steller Smith, a canary that Olivia-Ann has released from its cage. Sylvester silences Olivia-Ann and turns aside to the reader. He says, triumphantly: "Remember Mrs. Harry Steller Smith?" (202). He begs the reader to side with him and uses the rhetorical question in the same way that Sister does, to win the sympathy of the reader. When Stella-Rondo says that her uncle looks like a fool in her kimono, Sister comes to his defense. "'Well, he looks as good as he can,' I says. 'As good as anybody in reason could'" (49). Stella-Rondo tells Uncle Rondo in a later scene that Sister has described him as "a fool in that pink kimono" (52). Sister responds, by asking the reader to pity her plight. "Do you remember who it was really said that?" (52).

IV

Capote might well have entitled his story "My Side of the Matter: Or, Do You Remember Who It Was Really Said That?" His imitation of Welty and his denial of literary influence put him in an interesting position. His comments to Grobel suggest that a writer who bonds himself to tradition loses his identity and becomes psychotic, but his refusal to identify the source of his own work seems equally perverse. Capote's alterations of the earlier story reveal more clearly than the similarities that he struggles to resolve this paradox. "My Side of the Matter" transforms the narrator into an alter ego of the author and turns the antagonists into a successive string of females, who challenge Sylvester. The plot now centers on the accusation of theft—by a man, from a woman. The struggles between Sylvester and the women in Admiral's Mill have their counterpart in the acceptance and refusal of Welty as the original source, and represent the anxiety of female influence, which Capote must overcome.

The reassignment of sex roles in the second story turns the battle between Sylvester and the opposition into a gender issue. Sister faces off against a series of enemies who are equally distributed between the male and female sex—against Papa-Daddy and Uncle Rondo on the one hand, and Stella-Rondo and Mama on the other. Capote turns the conflict between the narrator and the other characters into a battle between the sexes. Sylvester now confronts Eunice, Olivia-Ann, Bluebell, and eventually Marge in a series of encounters that test his manhood. He asserts his authority by insisting that he has a position of patriarchal importance at the Cash'n'Carry, by defending his ability to impregnate his wife, and by demanding to sleep with her. The women attempt to separate Sylvester from the rest of the house because of his sexual status. Eunice says: "Birds setting in their roost—time we went to bed. You have your old room, Marge, and I've fixed a cot for this gentleman on the back porch" (200). The women are horrified by the possibility that Sylvester could assert the male prerogative, impregnate his wife, and work on her affections. They seek to castrate the protagonist, who finds an alternate means of asserting his sexual strength. Sylvester describes the influence of Eunice over Marge, and his attempt to counteract it.

> She has turned that girl against me in the most villainous fashion that words could not describe. Why, she even reached the point when she was sassing me back, but I provided her with a couple of good slaps and put a stop to that. No wife of mine is ever going to be disrespectful to me, not on your life! (201)

When he learns that he can't control his wife as a sexual male, he turns to force and seeks to assert his power, as a member of the "stronger" sex. He exerts physical power over other women in the house as well. As the battle progresses, he picks a parasol off of the hat tree and raps Bluebell "across the head with it until it cracked in two" (204). He describes himself as a victor in the sexual sense—as a "man." Only Sylvester has the strength to barricade himself behind the parlor door with "that big mahogany table that must weigh a couple of tons" (205). And only Sylvester can appropriate sexual power—pick and choose between Marge and "a five-pound box of Sweet Love candy" (205) that becomes a mock-romantic substitute for the female companion.

Sylvester creates a history for himself and other characters by building a sexual hierarchy that subordinates women and defines people by establishing their patriarchal roots. He undermines female influence by attributing the importance of Eunice and Olivia-Ann to the appropriation of masculine power. "There is a big table in one corner of the parlor which supports two pictures of Miss E and O-A's mama and papa. Papa ... was a captain in the Civil War" (202). The male tradition empowers the past and enables the narrator to live for the future. Sylvester says: "Oh, if it wasn't for that little unborn George I would've been making dust tracks on the road, way before now" (200). Unlike Marge, Eunice, and Olivia-Ann, Sylvester has no parents or past, according to the narrative. He is completely self-created and, as the narrative progresses, the reader learns that he is also able to create little men in his own image. Sylvester determines that the unborn child is a boy, believes that it will grow to be a man, and decides to protect it until the man can protect himself. He names the child and confers upon it the attribute of male power. "George Far Sylvester is a name we've planned for the baby. Has a strong sound, don't you think?" (199). The "strength" of the male child is due to his distance from the female group, as the middle name "Far" suggests. The reader establishes the identity of Sylvester himself through a naming process in the narrative which is self-referential and gender-reflexive, within the male tradition. The narrator uses the reflexive pronoun "I" to refer to himself and withholds his name from the reader as he withholds his presence and power from the women, at the end of the narrative. Through the naming of George Far Sylvester, the reader learns to identify the narrator himself as Sylvester—to link the father and son together, through the patriarchal surname.

Eunice and Olivia-Ann acknowledge their "inferiority" by imitating men or assuming the costume and behavior of the opposite sex to achieve power. Eunice chases Sylvester with her father's Civil War sword—a comic, phallic symbol and a relic from the male world of war and bloodshed. Olivia-Ann "squats around most of the time whittling on a stick with her fourteen-inch hog knife" (198). Both she and Eunice brandish their weapons, wave them in the face of the protagonist, and challenge his potency. They represent a threat to the male and give him a "half-inch cut" (204) that harms him less than it hurts his masculine pride. Sylvester counters the authority of women, throughout the story, by telling the reader that Eunice and Olivia-Ann fail as men and function as comic, pathetic imitations of the real thing. Eunice "chews tobacco and tries to pretend so ladylike, spitting on the sly" (197). Olivia-Ann has a "mustache" (197). Sylvester portrays the women as sex-starved maiden aunts who envy Marge because they can't get a man for themselves. In the absence of actual men, they imitate the opposite sex and persecute Sylvester because he represents the real thing.

They mock his pretensions to manhood, as he mocks theirs. Eunice glories in the role of bread-winner and belittles Sylvester.

> Why don't the little heathen go out and get some honest work? ...
> If he was any sort of man you could call a man he'd be trying to
> put a crust of bread in that girl's mouth instead of stuffing his own
> off my vittles. (201)

Olivia-Ann pokes fun of his small size and bad back, and refers to him as a "runt" (198). Both women devalue the man by denigrating his capacity to procreate and defining his status as a sexual failure. Olivia-Ann echoes her sister when she says that "he isn't even of the male sex" (198). "How can a girl have a baby with a girl?" (199). References to impotence and castration proliferate throughout the text and testify to the capacity of women to disarm their male opponents. Sylvester compares the tyranny of Eunice, in the community of Admiral's Mill, to the alleged rape of a woman by an elderly man.

> ... if she said Charlie Carson (a blind, ninety-year old invalid who
> hasn't taken a step since 1896) threw her on her back and raped
> her everybody in this county would swear the same on a stack of
> Bibles. (197)

The sisters assert their presence in the house, as they do in the community. Sylvester finds that "the fancy man tore out of this house one afternoon like old Adolf Hitler was on his tail and leaped into his Ford coupé, never to be heard from again" (201). Olivia-Ann locates the source of the feud, below the belt, and gives Sylvester a terrific "knee punch" (204) before running into the yard and shouting:

> Mine eyes have seen the glory of the
>   coming of the lord;
> He is trampling out the vintage where
>   the grapes of wrath are stored. (204)

She brings the opponent to his knees—literally—and tramples the "grapes of wrath," neutering the man whose genitals threaten the women.

The conflict begins with the accusation of Eunice, early in the story. Sylvester says:

> I happened to find close to a thousand dollars hidden in a flower pot on the side porch. I didn't touch one cent, only Eunice says I stole a hundred-dollar bill which is a venomous lie from start to finish. (197)

Later, the accusation precipitates the final fight in the story.

> "Where is it?" says she. "Where's my hundred dollars that he made away with while my trusting back was turned?"
>
> "*This* is the straw that broke the camel's back," says I, but I was too hot and tired to get up.
>
> "That's not the only back that's going to be broke," says she, her bug eyes about to pop clear out of their sockets. (203)

The theft by a man, from a woman, summarizes the conflict between men and women and symbolizes the central theme of the story: female influence and the denial of it. Eunice proclaims the dependence of men upon her and threatens to break the back of a man whose body is weaker than hers. Sylvester maintains his innocence, first by fighting Eunice, then by pushing her out of the parlor. The final image is an answer to the accusation. Sylvester locks himself in the room, using his physical isolation to assert his actual innocence, and to demonstrate his independence.

V

Capote leaves the crime—and the issue of influence—unresolved at the end of the story. He allows the reader to suspect Sylvester and certainly means to suggest that the locked door is evidence of an empty assertion. The isolation of the protagonist cannot, in itself, absolve him of the crime or his complicity in it. The denials cannot function, on their own, as an adequate defense. Capote compares the confrontation between Eunice and Sylvester to an earlier scene of accusation and denial. Eunice meets Sylvester, when he first arrives, and tells Marge that he looks like the "runt of the litter." Sylvester says: "I've never been so taken back in my life! True, I'm slightly stocky, but then I haven't got my full growth yet" (198). Sylvester responds to the accusation with a weak defense. The reader dismisses the reasoning process of the protagonist and carries a skeptical reaction to Sylvester over into the final episode of accusation and denial. To this extent, Capote allows the reader to doubt Sylvester, to interpret the outcome of the story, and to care about it. But ultimately he undermines the issue of female influence by leaving it open-ended. He suggests that the plot is irrelevant and that the accusation of theft is simply one in a chain of petty incidents in the narrative, championed by ridiculous people. The interaction of characters and the complication of events create a diversion which subverts interpretation and subordinates the issue of female influence to the illustration of the spectacle itself.

> In an interview with *Playboy*, in March, 1968, Capote said: I've never been psychoanalyzed; I've never even consulted a psychiatrist. I now consider myself a mentally healthy person. I work out all my problems in my work.[12]

Capote seems to work out the problem of influence in "My Side of the Matter," using the battle between Sylvester and the women to illustrate his own anxiety. He imitates Welty and reveals this intent, by tipping his hat to tradition in the title of the story. "My Side of the Matter" might well read "My Response to Eudora Welty," for Sylvester's battle seems to reflect Capote's own involvement with his predecessor. But in his comments on his work—in conversations, writings, and interviews—Capote contradicts the blatant link between himself and earlier writers. The psychological search for his own identity, within the text, leads the reader to suspect that the struggle between two images of the author—the psychotic and the "mentally healthy person"—never resolves itself. Taken in context with the author's statements about tradition and the struggle to create a literary identity, "My Side of the Matter" ultimately remains a problematic work. Sylvester's retreat to the parlor parallels Sister's withdrawal to the post office and indicates the extent to which the author draws upon his literary model. But Sylvester's rebuttal, behind the locked door, mirrors the protestations of the author, who uses the image of the locked room to illustrate his own autonomy. Capote's story, therefore, represents an intriguing compromise: a testimonial to tradition and a denial of it.

NOTES

1. Edgar Allan Poe, "The Murders in the Rue Morgue," from *The Complete Tales and Poems of Edgar Allan Poe* (New York: Vintage Books, 1975), p. 147.

2. Ibid., p. 150.

3. Truman Capote, *Music for Chameleons* (New York: Random House, 1975), p. xi.

4. Lawrence Grobel, *Conversations with Capote* (New York: New American Library, 1985), p. 97.

5. Ibid., p. 116.

6. Ibid., p. 149.

7. Ibid., p. 52.

8. Capote, *Music for Chameleons*, p. xii.

9. Grobel, *Conversations with Capote*, p. 82.

10. Eudora Welty, "Why I Live at the P.O.," from *The Collected Stories of Eudora Welty* (New York: Harcourt Brace Jovanovich, 1980), p. 46. Further references to this story are from the same edition and are included, parenthetically, within the text.

11. Truman Capote, "My Side of the Matter," from *"The Grass Harp"* and *"A Tree of Night"* (New York: Signet Books, 1980), p. 205. Further references to this story are from the same edition and are included, parenthetically, within the text.

12. William L. Nance, *The Worlds of Truman Capote* (New York: Stein and Day, 1970), p. 53. I borrow this passage from an interview in *Playboy*, which Nance quotes.

ERIC HEYNE

Toward a Theory of Literary Nonfiction

What is a historical fact? A spent shell? A bombed-out building?
A pile of shoes? A victory parade? A long march? Once it has
been suffered it maintains itself in the mind of witness or victim,
and if it is to reach anyone else it is transmitted in words or on
film and it becomes an image, which, with other images,
constitutes a judgment. I am well aware that some facts, for
instance the Nazi extermination of the Jews, are so indisputably
monstrous as to seem to stand alone. But history shares with
fiction a mode of mediating the world for the purpose of
introducing meaning, and it is the cultural authority from which
they both derive that illuminates those facts so that they can be
perceived.

E. L. Doctorow, "False Documents"

W hat do we mean when we contend that a nonfiction narrative is
literary? This question has become increasingly important in light of
excellent writing by Norman Mailer, Tom Wolfe, Michael Herr, and others,
and in response to literary historians, such as Robert Scholes and David
Lodge, who argue that our cultural aesthetic is demanding texts that define
"reality" and "realism" in new ways. Critical attention to the New Journalism

From *Modern Fiction Studies* 33, no. 3 (Autumn 1987). © 1987 by the Purdue Research
Foundation.

has succeeded in increasing our understanding and appreciation of particular works, but there remains a great deal of confusion about theoretical issues, such as the distinction between fact and fiction, the qualities of literary status in nonfiction, and the responsibilities of the author in turning history into art. Much of the confusion comes from terms such as "nonfiction novel," grandiose assertions such as "there is no difference between fiction and nonfiction," and simple-minded definitions of artistic nonfiction based on the use of techniques common in fiction. In this essay I will argue that literary nonfiction and fiction are fundamentally different, despite their resemblances in structure or technique, and that this difference must be recognized by any theory that hopes to do justice to powerful nonfiction narratives.

In "The Logical Status of Fictional Discourse" John Searle points out that the distinction we commonly make between factual and fictional statements is based, not on any characteristic of the statements themselves, but on our perception of the kind of statement being intended. Suppose a friend tells an amazing anecdote. If we believe it to be a joke or an invention, we look for a punchline or narrative flourishes; if we think it is a true story, we may formulate questions in our minds, asking for supplementary information. The proper response is indicated by the type of story we think we are being told, and that decision in turn is influenced by factors such as our relationship with the storyteller, the social context, and the antecedent conversation, as well as by properties of the story itself. We may not be sure what kind of story we are hearing, in which case we prepare for a joke so as to avoid being duped into treating invention as fact. In any event, we can never know purely on internal evidence whether the story is meant to be taken as true. Perhaps the teller is insane, in which case he may intend his story to be taken seriously, though our inclination is to doubt it. In that doubt lies a clue to the difference between fiction and nonfiction. It would not make sense to "doubt" a work of fiction. When we claim that something is a "true story," we mean either that it is to be taken in a certain way or that it can serve as an adequate representation of real events. The madman's tale is "true" in the first sense, but not in the second. The first distinction is between fact and fiction, the second between good and bad fact. This difference is important because, as the example of the anecdote illustrates, different sorts of responses are appropriate for fiction and nonfiction.

If Searle's distinction makes sense, it follows that the author is sole determinant of whether a text is fact or fiction, whereas the reader must decide for herself whether a work is good or bad fact. I will use the terms "factual status" and "factual adequacy" to distinguish between these two different kinds of truth. A fictional text has neither factual status nor factual adequacy; a nonfiction text has factual status, but readers would have to resolve individually or by debate the question of its factual adequacy. Status is either/or, a binary matter determined by "the illocutionary intentions of the author" (325), whereas adequacy is a relative matter open to debate between readers.

As long as we are talking about anecdotes, the problem remains relatively simple. The issue of an appropriate response is much more complicated when we start looking at longer stories, such as ambitious or experimental works of nonfiction. As a case study for this essay I will use Truman Capote's *In Cold Blood: A True Account of a Multiple Murder and Its Consequences*. In subtitle, Acknowledgements, and interviews Capote claimed that the book was "immaculately factual" (Plimpton 26).[1] There is little doubt that he wanted his book to have factual status, and most readers have taken *In Cold Blood* as nonfiction. However, there is a strong tendency among critics to talk about the book as a kind of novel. This tendency is based, oddly enough, on two very different evaluations of the book. Some critics argue that *In Cold Blood* is radically inaccurate, and so should be labeled "fiction," whereas others so admire its dramatic power that they want to grant it honorary status as a novel. Analyzing these two positions may help clarify the notions of factual status and factual adequacy and explain their usefulness in a theory of literary nonfiction.

Perhaps the most interesting reaction to the publication of *In Cold Blood* was Philip K. Tompkins' research into the events of the book. His article, "In Cold Fact," details the discrepancies he found, places where Capote deliberately or accidentally departed from the actual events so far as Tompkins could determine them. Though he is willing to grant Capote the benefit of every doubt, Tompkins concludes that at the very least Capote put his own observations into the mouths and minds of other characters, and at the worst he created a mixed-up, inaccurate portrait of the murderer Perry Smith:

> For premeditated murder performed in cold blood, Capote substituted unpremeditated murder performed in a fit of insanity. Art triumphs over reality, fiction over nonfiction. By imparting conscience and compassion to Perry, Capote was able to convey qualities of inner sensitivity, poetry, and a final posture of contrition in his hero. The killer cries. He asks to have his hand held. He says, "I'm embraced by shame." He apologizes. It is a moving portrait but not, I submit, of the man who actually was

Perry Smith—the man who, in real life, told his friend Cullivan he was *not* sorry, the same man who would not play the hypocrite with Cullivan or his old friend Willie-Jay. (57)

If Capote did indeed "create" Perry Smith, that decision has important consequences for our evaluation of *In Cold Blood*, because critics have generally agreed that Smith is the protagonist of the book and that one of Capote's central aims is indicated by the intended irony of the title: it is Smith rather than the Clutter family who is killed "in cold blood."[2]

If Capote's book were a novel, Tompkins' research would, of course, be impossible. Because it is nonfiction, however, competing accounts are relevant, perhaps even vital. How factually adequate is *In Cold Blood*, and how important is the answer to that question in deciding on the value of the book? Melvin J. Friedman believes that Capote "cheated" but that his doing so does not matter much: "Despite the convincing claims of unreliability ... we must still believe in the essential authenticity and integrity of Capote's account" (168). Unfortunately, Friedman does not go into detail about what constitutes "the essential authenticity and integrity" of the book, nor about how that may be preserved in the face of inaccuracies. If one believes, on the other hand, that Capote's "cheating" weakened his book (primarily through sentimentalizing his protagonist), what is the appropriate response? For Tompkins, it is to conclude that "art triumphs over reality, fiction over nonfiction."

In the terms of our analysis, Tompkins reasons from factual inadequacy to fictional status. Ignoring Capote's intentions, Tompkins decides to read all or part of *In Cold Blood* as fiction. This is the same move as labeling an exposed hoax, such as the "Hitler diaries," a fiction, in the common use of the word to describe anything false. But for the purposes of literary criticism do we really want a definition of fiction that includes discredited narratives of fact, such as lies, misguided histories, and unethical journalism? I would prefer Searle's more precise distinction between works intended to be read and evaluated as fiction, and works intended to be read and evaluated as fact. A corollary of this position is that one can never move backward from a decision about factual adequacy to any determination of factual or fictional status. This makes it easier to see that Tompkins is doing a disservice to "art" by relegating to it whatever errors Capote may have made. If Capote seriously misrepresented the character of Perry Smith, the result is not a triumph of "fiction over nonfiction," but of lying over truth-telling, or blindness over insight.

There is more involved in Tompkins' position, however, than just a different use of the word "fiction." Undercutting the value of his own investigations, Tompkins concludes that *In Cold Blood* is a "work of art" that will be enjoyed "for its own sake" long after the "discrepancies of fact" have been forgotten (58). Unlike Friedman, Tompkins believes that the book's inaccuracies are central, but, like Friedman, Tompkins believes that the book is good enough to survive as literature, though metamorphosed into fiction. It may be easy to accept this claim, because *In Cold Blood* is a skillfully-constructed narrative, and very much like many novels in its structure, style, and effects. However, I believe there is another kind of confusion involved here: this time it is not between factual status and factual adequacy but between fictional status and literary merit.

In his study of literary nonfiction, *Fables of Fact*, John Hellmann argues that "the new journalist presents fact in fictional form, but it is fiction only in the more sophisticated and original sense of the word that has led Northrop Frye to apply it to 'any work of art in prose'" (17). Frye's use of the term may have been "original," but he is now one of many critics who have suggested that traditional literary genres be conflated into a larger category, such as literary discourse. As Frye and Hellmann use "fiction," it becomes merely a synonym for literary prose and leaves us without a way to distinguish between fiction and nonfiction. To quote Searle again, "the concept of literature is a different concept from that of fiction. Thus, for example, 'the Bible as literature' indicates a theological neutral attitude, but 'the Bible as fiction' is tendentious" (320). Hellmann is correct when he observes that "we think of the works of Capote, Mailer, Wolfe, Herr, Thompson, and other new journalists as members of a single genre, despite their being spread throughout the Library of Congress ..." (24). However, I would argue that part of the reason we would group them together would be to *separate* them from novels, as nonfiction narratives of such power and complexity that they deserve the attention of literary critics.

Hellmann's argument for "The New Journalism as New Fiction," as he puts it in his subtitle, is based upon Frye's notion that texts have a "final direction," determined either by "relation to the external world" or by a "form" that finally "points to" itself (23-24). This model suggests that a text must lose touch with the "external world" insofar as it develops an engaging form. It follows that good historical writing must either approach fiction or remain aesthetically displeasing in form. But where does that leave the historiographers who are interested in the union of form and fact in good history?

> historiography is like the novel in being itself our experience of
> what it narrates.... The experience of the past represented thus
> depends, in part, on the presentational skill of the historian and
> on his aesthetic judgment (van den Haag 223).[3]

> the best grounds for choosing one perspective on history rather
> than another are ultimately aesthetic or moral rather than
> epistemological ... (White, *Metahistory* xii).

Recalling Searle's example, we may find it useful to talk about "history as literature," but tendentious or even malicious to talk about "history as fiction." Fiction and nonfiction are both narrative and may share all sorts of technical similarities in their constructions of meaning. But it is the rankest sort of critical imperialism to use comparison between the two to appropriate good journalism rather than to clarify our understanding of good writing of both kinds.

In *The Mythopoeic Reality* Mas'ud Zavarzadeh has attacked the fact/fiction distinction from the more radical position that "the epistemological crisis of our 'age of suspicion'" has rendered the whole notion of fact versus fiction obsolete (41). According to Zavarzadeh, the "fictuality" of contemporary life has produced narratives that cannot be taken as either factual or fictional but only as somehow both simultaneously. Like Hellmann, Zavarzadeh employs a model of narrative based on "direction" inward or outward, toward the self-contained world of the narrative or the confusing, largely nonverbal world of real events. Where he differs is in his characterization of the "nonfiction novel" as a narrative balanced between the two directions, with no final allegiance to either the inner or the outer world. The appeal of his argument is that it seems to explain the difficulty people have making decisions about truth. Every narrative is a version, and there are not always firm principles for judging all versions, nor enough information available to make satisfying decisions about representational accuracy. The modern reader in search of narrative truth cannot trust newspapers, must weigh competing historical accounts, and often ends up deciding that a story is more or less true, rather than just true or false. Zavarzadeh suggests that we will have to abandon the fact/fiction distinction in the face of increasingly complex modes of telling applied to an increasing amount of information. This is an interesting piece of advice, but it certainly is not a description of what people do. We commonly depend on distinguishing between fact and fiction, employing our "factual competence," as it were. When we are challenged by a narrative that presents itself as fact, but includes dialogue or events that we may doubt, our response is usually to challenge the text and determine its worth, not throw up our hands and surrender. We will continue to maintain the fact/fiction distinction at least as long as we find it worthwhile to conduct a collective search for the truths of our past.[4]

One of the consequences of factual status is that it brings into play certain epistemological principles, variously codified for the different purposes of journalism, history, and law. When we pick up a work of nonfiction, we have in mind questions about access to information, first- and second-hand sources, and so on. If the text is clearly a piece of journalism, a history, or a courtroom transcript, we can narrow the appropriate responses even farther. However, in the case of an ambitious or experimentaltext, we will not be able to decide ahead of time which epistemological principles are to be in force—unless we privilege certain conventions. This is exactly what John Hersey does when he applies to the work of Norman Mailer, Tom Wolfe, and Truman Capote the strict standards of journalism. Not surprisingly, Hersey concludes that his fellow authors are poor reporters: "The writer of fiction must invent. The journalist must not invent" (25). This neat aphorism is entirely correct, as long as it is intended only as part of a description of conventional journalistic practice. However, conventions are made to be challenged, in nonfiction as in fiction. As literary critics we have a special interest in innovation, and it makes more sense for us to begin reading with an open mind, discovering along the way which conventions will be adhered to and which ignored or tested by a particular text.

This does not mean that an author can get away with anything he pleases or can expect us to believe everything he says. I think that Capote damaged *In Cold Blood* by violating certain conventions of accurate presentation. But that belief is based on the conviction that Capote did not abide by his *own* rules, the principles which he indicates in his text to be in force. For instance, he employs an omniscient point of view, telling his story from the perspectives of a variety of characters but never entering the narrative as a character or making explicit value judgments as a narrator. He strongly implies that one or more of his characters provide firsthand evidence for every event and that words placed in quotation marks can be verified to virtually everyone's satisfaction. However, Tompkins found witnesses to dispute Capote's version of some of Smith's "exact words," including his final apology. A moving scene from the book appears not to have happened as Capote tells it:[5]

> During our telephone conversation, Mrs. Meier repeatedly told
> me that she *never* heard Perry cry; that on the day in question she
> was in her bedroom, not the kitchen; that she did not turn on the
> radio to drown out the sound of crying; that she did not hold
> Perry's hand; that she did not hear Perry say, "I'm embraced by
> shame." And finally—that she had never told such things to
> Capote. Mrs. Meier told me repeatedly and firmly, in her gentle
> way, that these things were not true. (Tompkins 53)

Either Capote completely made up key scenes, or he transferred his own
experiences to another character. In either case he violated the principles he
set up for himself in this book, reducing his accomplishments considerably.
However, this does not mean that Capote made up all of *In Cold Blood* or that
any nonfiction writer who makes up scenes would be cheating, or that
Capote must have intended me to read his book without regard to whether
he made things up. Factual status is crucial to the experience of reading *In
Cold Blood*, which in turn means that we are invited to make a decision about
its factual adequacy, not merely according to *a priori* principle but by the
rules Capote indicates are in force in his book.

We might tentatively identify two different kinds of truth—accuracy
and meaning—for which different principles are important. The former
involves a kind of groundwork, a detailed and sufficiently neutral verbal
representation of events, for which the goal is universal agreement or
correspondence. The latter is much more nebulous, covering virtually
everything one does with "the facts" once they have been given an accurate
shape. In practice there is seldom any convenient way to distinguish a fact
from its meaning, because facts are verbal models that always already
participate in the infinite connotations of language. Moreover, facts can be
variously broad, complex, and controversial, just as meanings can.
Nevertheless, and without pretending to any sort of philosophical
profundity, I think we can usefully talk about accuracy and meaning as
different sorts of claims or strategies in nonfiction narrative.

We judge competition between true stories to be important because we
believe that two people witnessing the same event could eventually come up
with some shared version of that event, a linguistic model to which both
would accede. There are so many variables in play—differences in sensory
acuteness, perspective and other contextual factors, memory and conceptual
skills, available vocabulary, and so on—that it is a wonder people ever agree
on a version of anything. Fortunately, language is so flexible a tool that in
daily life we manage to agree well enough on versions of just about

everything, or at least on the kind of information that, if available, would produce such agreement. In the competition between Capote's and Tompkins' versions of events in Kansas, our concern thus far has been accuracy. Capote did not achieve the "immaculate" correspondence to events that he claimed. However, it is the influence of his inaccuracies upon the meaning of the book that is fatal. Complex truths may be well served by inventions, exaggerations, slanting, and other transformations of fact. But in the case of *In Cold Blood*, the inventions concern the character of Perry Smith, and his precise motivations are at the thematic and aesthetic heart of the book. Capote's meaning is flawed by his inaccuracies. If they had not been exposed by Tompkins, *In Cold Blood* would be a more important book, not merely for historical reasons, but aesthetically as well.

We have arrived at the issue of literary value, albeit by a very strange route. This whole discussion of accuracy and competition runs counter to the traditional notion of literary value as transcendent or a-contextual. As John M. Ellis puts it, "literary texts are defined as those that are used by the society in such a way that *the text is not taken as specifically relevant to the immediate context of its origin*" (44). I am generally in agreement with Ellis' "performance" definition of literature: "Literary texts are not defined as those of a certain shape or structure, but as those pieces of language used in a certain way by the community" (42). However, I want to take issue with the claim that "the community" always divorces the literary text from "the immediate context of its origin." In fact, I would argue that virtually everyone is interested in the origins of texts—in questions about authors, dates, influences, careers, and so forth—notwithstanding the fact that many critics, for various philosophical or rhetorical reasons, play down such matters in their writing and teaching. I think it would be more accurate to amend Ellis by saying that literary texts are not taken as *limited* in relevance or significance by the details of their origins.

What about *In Cold Blood*? To put it baldly, is it literature or not? This question, which I have frequently encountered in casual discussions about the book, is extremely frustrating because it indicates the degree to which an essentialist theory of literary value is alive and well. In order for me to participate in a discussion of the literariness of *In Cold Blood*, I first have to explain the view of Ellis, Searle, and others, that literature is a "family resemblance" notion and that members are certified over time. As Searle puts it, "the literary is continuous with the nonliterary. Not only is there no sharp boundary, but there is not much of a boundary at all" (320). What good would it do to state flatly that *In Cold Blood* will or will not be taught in a few years? A more honest and more helpful version of that frustrating question is, what is valuable about Capote's book? Put another way, to make the connection between the two versions clearer, upon what grounds could one argue that *In Cold Blood* deserves literary status? Looking at the issue this way foregrounds the reader's role in the fluid (especially for contemporary works) question of literary status, without, I hope, taking the responsibility for that status out of the author's hands entirely.

The corollary to a performance definition of literature is that there are no universal criteria for literary value. But what about within a particular genre? Is it possible to discover the essence of literary value in nonfiction narrative, to derive a principle for admitting true stories into the canon? Surely we can agree that literary nonfiction creates absorbing, convincing patterns from the material of verifiable facts:

> to the degree that any factual narrative is responded to as literature, its form may be analyzed as inherently the cause of an effect. And insofar as the form has the capacity to produce an effect, it will have raised human fact out of contingency and made it concretely present as a striking but inherently probable manifestation of complete and morally determinate human thought, character, or action, individual or collective. (Rader 38)[6]

The problem with this eloquent assertion by Ralph Rader is that it is finally just a sophisticated and apparently democratic statement of a certain classical taste in narrative, *not*, as I might devoutly wish it to be, a genuinely empirical definition of literary value in nonfiction. There are some texts that are literature (at least according to some critics) but that make only minimal gestures in the direction of "complete and morally determinate human thought, character, or action." Other arguably literary texts emphasize rather than explode the "contingency" in "human fact" or present real life in ways that make it less than "concretely present." Moreover, how do we know that future texts we will want to call "literature" will not violate some or all of the clauses of Rader's literary contract? I put a fair amount of time into my own search for the characteristic pleasure of literary nonfiction (example: the dual satisfaction of specific truth-claims and profound or vivid patterns) before I faced up to the idealist assumption motivating that search. There is no way to get from "What I find valuable about *In Cold Blood*" to "What is valuable about all nonfiction narrative."

In order to explore the consequences of this unavoidable aporia, I want to return to the issue of factual adequacy, in particular its relationship with literary status. I have already argued that inaccuracy is not necessarily fatal to a nonfiction text; neither, of course, does accuracy guarantee a work of literature—witness the tons of newsprint and volumes of history that never tempt the literary critic to exercise his skills upon them. Moreover, there is never one version of any event that is the best for all purposes. For instance, Hunter Thompson's *Fear and Loathing: On the Campaign Trail '72* and Norman Mailer's *St. George and the Godfather* cover many of the same events and describe many of the same people, but the relative success of one does not detract from the other. They are competing accounts but with different purposes and different forms. No single event can ever be drained of its meaning, any more than a careful presentation of that event in words will ensure a profound meaning. In order to evaluate a complex nonfiction narrative, it is essential to understand the exact truth-claims being made and how they fit into the author's overall intentions.[7]

The preceding analysis may have appeared to be employing a very naive view of the relationship between language and experience, as though accuracy were a simple thing that one could decide to achieve or ignore. I certainly did not mean to imply that such was the case. Many theorists of narrative argue that there is an enormous gap between any event and any linguistic version of that event. Historiographers in particular have been talking a lot about the unavoidable abstractions of their craft:

> I have sought to suggest that this value attached to narrativity in the representation of real events arises out of a desire to have real events display the coherence, integrity, fullness, and closure of an image of life that is and can only be imaginary. (White, "Value" 27)

> Though it makes use of things that have actually happened rather than inventions, history writing is merely another way of satisfying the rage for formal satisfaction. (Toliver 52)

In brief, there is no transcendent connection between space/time events and narratives of those events; all factual narratives are versions, "constructed, as *all* versions are, by someone in particular, on some occasion, for some purpose, and in accord with some relevant set of principles" (Smith 218).

However, recognizing that we are students of human constructions shaped by human purposes need not make us afraid to talk about truth. We make decisions every day based on our evaluations of competing versions of reality. Just because we are without absolute rules universally accepted for the construction of accurate or meaningful narrative, we do not have to conclude that therefore we cannot claim that one story is truer than another. We just have to be careful, look at specific cases, and make explicit the standards by which we are judging truth. This is one contribution of the model of factual status and factual adequacy: it allows us to narrow the grounds for certain kinds of inquiry and thereby to arrive more quickly at helpful questions.

Another virtue of this theory is that it strives for a shared understanding of the nature of texts that serve multiple functions in society. I do not wish to suggest chauvinistically that more of the world can be saved by nonfiction than by fiction, merely that the problems of finding a communal truth make the study of literary nonfiction particularly exciting. As technology gathers information from farther and farther afield, we will continue to look for authors who can find striking, enduring patterns for that unwashed mass of facts. I think it is important to frame our discussion of literary nonfiction in terms that recognize its potential success as both a useful model of reality and an aesthetically pleasing verbal pattern of human meanings.

NOTES

1. I chose Capote's book for this essay because it has been widely read and discussed and because Philip K. Tompkins' research provides a rare instance of a strong competing account.

2. In support of this reading, critics most frequently cite the comment of the "young reporter from Oklahoma" (343).

3. Note the similarity of van den Haag's phrase, "itself our experience of what it narrates," to Hellmann's characterization of fiction as narrative in which the "elements of the text create relations establishing an experience in the text" (24).

4. There are certainly instances in which the factual status of a text is problematic, either because the author's intentions are not clear or because those intentions involve experimenting with the fact/fiction distinction. But even experimentation is defined by a norm from which to deviate. Zavarzadeh does not seem to recognize the difference between challenging conventions and simply abolishing them.

5. The scene in question is on p. 345 of *In Cold Blood*.

6. Donald Pizer argues a similar position (207).

7. The observation that every work of literary nonfiction must establish its own factual adequacy certainly does not imply that therefore nonfiction narratives can be ranked by bulk of detail, profundity of theme, or historical

importance of their topics. Critics can no more privilege a particular kind of factual adequacy as the determinant of literary value than they can decide that a particular type of mimesis or theme or style is *the* standard of value in fiction.

Works Cited

Ellis, John M. *The Theory of Literary Criticism: A Logical Analysis.* Berkeley: U of California P, 1974.

Friedman, Melvin. "Towards an Aesthetic: Truman Capote's Other Voices." Malin 163-176.

Hellmann, John. *Fables of Fact: The New Journalism as New Fiction.* Urbana: U of Illinois P, 1981.

Hersey, John. "The Legend on the License." *Yale Review* 70 (1980): 1-25.

Malin, Irving, ed. *Truman Capote's "In Cold Blood": A Critical Handbook.* Belmont: Wadsworth, 1968.

Pizer, Donald. "Documentary Narrative as Art: William Manchester and Truman Capote." *The Reporter as Artist: A Look at the New Journalism Controversy.* Ed. Ronald Weber. New York: Hastings, 1974. —207-219.

Plimpton, George. "The Story Behind a Nonfiction Novel." Malin 25-43.

Rader, Ralph W. "Literary Form in Factual Narrative: The Example of Boswell's 'Johnson.'" *Essays in Eighteenth-Century Biography.* Ed. Philip B. Daghlian. Bloomington: U of Illinois P, 1968.3-42.

Searle, John. "The Logical Status of Fictional Discourse." *New Literary History* 6 (1975): 319-332.

Smith, Barbara Herrnstein. "Narrative Versions, Narrative Theories." *Critical Inquiry* 7 (1980): 213-236.

Toliver, Harold. *Animate Illusions: Explorations of Narrative Structure.* Lincoln: U of Nebraska P, 1974.

Tompkins, Philip K. "In Cold Fact." Malin 44-58.

van den Haag, Ernest. "History as Factualized Fiction." *Philosophy and History: A Symposium.* Ed. Sidney Hook. New York: New York UP, 1963. 212-226.

White, Hayden. *Metahistory: The Historical Imagination in Nineteenth-Century Europe.* Baltimore: Johns Hopkins UP, 1973.

————. "The Value of Narrativity in the Representation of Reality." *Critical Inquiry* 7 (1980): 5-27.

own destinies and tell their own stories"—he gives "the illusion that he is sitting silently behind scenes" of the story itself (7, 273, 50).

Silence in this sense is also related to Wolfgang Iser's notion that the reading experience depends on "gaps" or "blanks," the gaps arising from dialogue, for example, or from unexplained events, delayed revelations, and uninterpreted concrete images. At these junctures, "what *is* said only appears to take on significance as a reference to what is not said; it is the implications and not the statements themselves that give shape and weight to the meaning" (168). In the space left by the withdrawal of the narrator, meaning takes place. Information withheld, interpretation withdrawn, the reader is left to draw inferences and make connections.

In *Other Voices, Other Rooms*, for example, Capote's first and perhaps most representative novel, the narrator is silent for most of the story about Joel's father. Joel has come to Skully's Landing to live with a father he has never known, but from the beginning of his stay no one will tell him anything about the man—where he is, what he is like, when he can see him:

> "Miss Amy," he said, as they started down the stairs, "where is
> my dad? I mean, couldn't I see him, please, ma'am?"
> She did not answer. (50)

As narrator Capote doesn't answer this question either. He deliberately withholds information and interpretation throughout the first half of the novel. We know no more than Joel. With him we must explore the strange, silent house and deal with its enigmatic inhabitants—Randolph, Miss Amy—drawing what conclusions we can. At one point Joel hears a strange thumping on the stairs. It stops, there is "an instant of quiet," "then an ordinary red tennis ball roll[s] silently through the archway" (87). Later we find that this is a signal from Joel's invalid father for Randolph or Amy to come upstairs, but at this point it is a strange, mysterious sign, silent and uninterpreted. Like many other events and details in the novel, it puzzles Joel and it puzzles us. Capote leaves us with Joel to work out its significance.

Just as importantly, silence has to do with the way Capote dramatizes rather than explicates his central themes, relying on symbolism, the implications of concreteness, to convey meaning. He shows rather than tells. In the conclusion of *Other Voices* Joel stands in the garden at Skully's Landing and looks up at the clouds:

> The clouds traveled slower than a clock's hands, and, as he
> waited, became thunder-dark, became John Brown and horrid

boys in panama hats and the Cloud Hotel and Isabel's old hound, and when they were gone, Mr. Sansom was the sun.

There is a sense of anticipation now. Something, some revelation, is about to take place:

> His mind was absolutely clear. He was like a camera waiting for its subject to enter focus. The wall yellowed in the meticulous setting of the October sun, and the windows were rippling mirrors of cold, seasonal color. Beyond one, someone was watching him. All of him was dumb except his eyes. They knew. And it was Randolph's window. Gradually the blinding sunset drained from the glass, darkened, and it was as if snow were falling there, flakes shaping snow-eyes, hair: a face trembled like a white beautiful moth, smiled. She beckoned to him, shining and silver, and he knew he must go: unhurried, not hesitating, he paused only at the garden's edge where, as though he'd forgotten something, he stopped and looked back at the bloomless, descending blue, at the boy he had left behind. (230-31)

Many threads of symbolism and implication developed from the beginning of the novel come together here, too complicated to explicate now. For our purposes it is enough to note that Capote does not explicitly comment on Joel's rite of passage. The moment is fundamentally symbolic, rendered concretely rather than openly interpreted. We must *read* the detail. On one level Joel is leaving the garden of his youthful innocence. On another he has learned the importance of passively accepting the darkness around him as the only way of escaping that darkness. He has come to see his father, Mr. Sansom, free of the clouds that have always surrounded him. He has come to accept Randolph, his sexually ambiguous cousin, who apparently is the mysterious woman he has repeatedly glimpsed in the upstairs window. In the moment in the garden, a moment where nothing essentially "happens" in any external sense—where everything, in fact, is literally silent—Joel moves from boyhood to manhood, although in Capote's rich silence it is unclear how full or healthy this manhood will be.

As in all literary expression, it is the concrete details of the dramatized situation that carry the weight of meaning. Capote does not "say" what he means here. What he says is the scene itself; what he means is what the scene implies, points to, causes us to think about for ourselves. This is the strategy in all of Capote's fiction, from the early stories—like "Miriam" and "The

the character of Dick and Perry and detailing the reaction of the townspeople to the murder. Throughout this long intervening section he remains silent about the central event of the narrative.

As a result, we must join Alvin Dewey, the detective in charge of the case, as he struggles to decipher clues. With him we must try to account for the position of the bodies, the nature of the wounds, the state of the house. In the absence of answers, we must form hypotheses. It's "like those puzzles," Dewey himself puts it, "the ones that ask, 'How many animals can you find in this picture?'" (83). The animals are hidden for us precisely because of Capote's authorial silence. He doesn't tell us what he knows.

Capote continually puts us in the position of reading externals, even in the most apparently trivial scenes. Mrs. Clutter's room is austere, without personal ornament, "as though by keeping this room impersonal, by not importing her intimate belongings but leaving them mingled with those of her husband, she lessened the offense of not sharing his quarters" (29). The handwriting in Nancy's diary varies from entry to entry, sometimes slanted to the right, sometimes to the left, sometimes round, sometimes steep, "as though she were asking, 'Is this Nancy? Or that? Or that? Which is me?'" (57). "As though" conjectures are a necessary response to silence. Without the certainty of fact we can only deduce internals from the character of externals. Even near the end, when Perry is captured and brought in for questioning, Capote chooses to present him to us from a distance. With the detectives we view him through the one-way observation window of the interrogation room, deducing what we can from his "stiff Indian Hair," his "pert, impish features," his flickering, lizard-like tongue (224).

It is from this perspective that we can understand the symbolic resonances characteristic of *In Cold Blood*. The cats who fish through the gutters for dead birds outside the courthouse are meant to be symbolic of people within the story—Dick and Perry, the journalists coming to cover the murder (258). Capote notes that over a Las Vegas motel where the police are searching for the killers an "R" and the "S" are missing from "rooms." The truncated word "OOM" seems to resonate in the rest of the story, a symbol of the disintegration of language and meaning in the face of violence (174). Earlier in this section Capote records part of a radio broadcast that awakens a prisoner in the Kansas State Penitentiary ("Chancellor Konrad Adenauer arrived in London today for talks with Prime Minister Harold Macmillan.... President Eisenhower put in seventy minutes going over space problems and the budget for space exploration with Dr. T. Keith Glennan"), subtly linking the events that took place in Holcomb, Kansas, with world events on the eve of a new decade. These details are all presumably "true," yet selected from their context they assume a symbolic, evocative value beyond their literal meaning. As in Capote's fiction, concreteness does not mean what it says; it points beyond itself, evokes via association or metaphor something not stated.

In his later nonfiction Capote continues to assume an objective point of view, only this time eschewing omniscience entirely and acknowledging the perceiving "I." In "Hello Stranger" (*Music for Chameleons*), he presents without commentary a conversation with a friend who confesses a strange sexual indiscretion. The sketch is constructed around the interview form itself—"TC's" question followed by "George's" answer—with a minimum of connecting description. The surface of the story and of the man who tells it are presented, without explicit interpretation, for us to judge. In "Handcarved Coffins," also a part of *Music For Chameleons*, Capote again features the bare skeleton of the interview, the give-and-take of question and answer without the narrator's all-seeing interventions. Occasionally he adds, in tight, almost minimalist parentheses, some description of the surrounding scene or landscape. There is never commentary. Here in these later pieces there are just the lineaments of the act of experiencing itself, the "I" in its immediate transactions with the world. By making himself nominally present in the story, Capote emphasizes silence even more than in *In Cold Blood*. Acknowledging the "I" in its act of observation calls our attention to the opaqueness of surfaces we must interpret for ourselves.

In an important statement in a *Paris Reviews* interview, Capote identifies this kind of rhetorical silence as the common strategy of both his fiction and his nonfiction:

> In reporting one is occupied with literalness and surfaces, with implication without comment—one can't achieve immediate depths the way one may in fiction. However, one of the reasons I've wanted to do reportage was to prove that I could apply my style to the realities of journalism. But I believe my fictional method is equally detached—emotionality makes me lose writing control: I have to exhaust the emotion before I feel clinical enough to analyze and project it, and as far as I'm concerned that's one of the laws of achieving true technique. (Nance, *The Worlds of Truman Capote*, 169).

In a sense the rhetoric of silence is more appropriate to nonfiction than to fiction. After all, in nonfiction the author cannot finally claim total omniscience. Capote can't say with absolute certainty why Nancy Clutter varies her handwriting, because she is a real person, not a fictional creation of his own. He can't say why Mrs. Clutter would keep her separate bedroom so austere, because he cannot read her mind. The rhetoric of silence acknowledges the limits of factual reporting. But at the same time Capote recognizes that the rhetoric of silence is the central strategy of his fiction (and, we would add, of most modern fiction). The technique of reading "surfaces" and making inferences from those surfaces is a choice for the novelist in a way it cannot be for the nonfiction writer, but its purposes and effects are the same in both modes. There is still the same insistence on the reader participating in the making of deductions, still the narrator's refusal to speak in his own voice and comment on the meaning of the action he has dramatized, the character he has described. The key to technique in both modes is "detachment"—control, distance, concreteness, the dramatization rather than explication of events. Both fiction and nonfiction depend, in this view, on "implication without comment."

Thus Capote's nonfiction has the same two contradictory rhetorical effects as his fiction. It elicits and at the same time demands a reading. It draws us into the narrative and at the same time makes it harder for us to understand the meaning of the words before us. Unlike more conventional narrative exposition, where everything is spelled out as completely as possible in its turn, Capote's nonfiction develops from implicitness, restraint, withholding. It is riddled with at least temporary moments of indeterminancy.

In this respect the rhetoric of silence in Capote's nonfiction is representative of the implicitness and restraint that characterizes all "literary nonfiction" or "New Journalism" or "nonfiction novels." Though we would not normally associate Tom Wolfe—in his verbosity and enthusiasm—with the notion of silence, his prose depends on what he calls the use of "scene-by-scene reconstruction" with as little "historical narration" as possible (*The New Journalism*, 31). That is, Wolfe dramatizes rather than explicates his topics, inhabiting the consciousness of his characters and for the most part withholding comment on events in his own voice. In terms of point of view, Wolfe is "silent" as a narrator, although his dense and rhetorically self-conscious style carries more than traces of his attitudes and opinions. The prose of Joan Didion is also characterized by a resolute fidelity to concrete detail unadorned with commentary. Her habitual strategy is to isolate the ironic or symbolic or evocative image and then let the image speak for itself. By temperament, she claims, she is incapable of thinking "in abstracts" or traveling in the "world of ideas." Her mind by its nature "veers inexorably back to the specific, the tangible," to "the physical fact." "You just lie low and let them develop," she says of such images. "You stay quiet" ("Why I Write," —178-79). Didion's prose is a succession of scenes, stories, dialogues, dramatized moments arranged with a minimum of connecting explication. What makes nonfiction fictive for both Wolfe and Didion, as for Capote, is the symbolic implications and patterns of meaning that emerge from the shaping and positioning of these concrete images. Capote's style is paradigmatic of contemporary American prose.

In a series of prefaces to his various collections of nonfiction, Capote has discussed his effort over a career to fashion a prose style of understatement and conciseness. He has striven, he says, for a "technical virtuosity as strong and flexible as a fisherman's net," a sentence structure "simple, clear as a country creek" ("Chameleons," xvii). This involves cutting and condensing, a radical revising away of what he perceives as the former "density" of his prose so that he can achieve the same effects in a single paragraph that he achieved before in three pages (vii). Or as he puts it in the preface to *The Dogs Bark*, he is struggling to control his "static" writing, "to reveal character and sustain mood unaided by a narrative line" (xviii), an interesting parallel to Wolfe's intention of developing narrative with as little "historical narration" as possible. In the terms I have been developing, it seems clear that what Capote is really describing here is the rhetoric of silence, an attempt to create language which means more than it says, which shows rather than tells, which depends in the end on the author's strategic decision to stay out of what is ultimately pure narration and description.

Capote says it best, perhaps, in a tribute to the style of Japanese art. In his view all Japanese art depends on the "dread of the explicit." Thus, "the single blade of grass describing a whole universe of summer, the slightly lowered eyes left to suggest the deepest passion." The withholding of interpretation, the restraining of comment, is "all a ceremony of Style, a phenomenon that seems to rotate, in a manner quite separate from emotional content, on absolute style alone" (*The Dogs Bark*, 356). This is a spare and understated piece in itself, no more than 500 words long, richer in implication than in analysis. It is a fitting critical analysis of the rhetoric of silence, even though the word "silence" is never mentioned. In Capote, too, a blade of grass is "left" to describe the whole universe of summer, lowered eyes left to suggest deeper realities of character. Looking back over Capote's career, it is easy to see how the excesses of his private life obscured the stylistic integrity such reticence demands. Now that Capote has died, it is time to put the work in its proper perspective, to acknowledge the technical virtuosity of these controlled and crafted resonances.

BIBLIOGRAPHY

Booth, Wayne C. *The Rhetoric of Fiction*. Chicago, 1961.
Capote, Truman. *The Dogs Bark*. New York, 1973.
———. *In Cold Blood*. New York, 1965.
———. *Music For Chameleons*. New York, 1980.
———. *Other Voices, Other Rooms*. New York, 1948.
———. *Selected Writings*. New York, 1963.
Didion, Joan. "Why I Write." In *Modern American Prose*. John Clifford and Robert Diyanni, eds. New York, 1983.
Iser, Wolfgang. *The Act of Reading*. Baltimore, 1978.
Nance, William. *The Worlds of Truman Capote*. New York, 1970.
Wolfe, Tom, ed. *The New Journalism*. New York, 1973.

HELEN S. GARSON

Those Were the Lovely Years

Capote's early work reveals a writer with two diametrically opposed styles. Although most of the early stories are about children or young adults, the different techniques reflect the polarity of his vision. One pattern, baring the dark and frightening shadows of existence, characterizes his gothic stories; the other reveals the joyful Capote who created stories of bright, brief, happy days that seem to hold promise and hope for the future. In three of the best-known and most successful examples of this lighthearted fiction—"Children on Their Birthdays," *The Grass Harp*, and *Breakfast at Tiffany's*,—the themes are clear, the young protagonists captivating, the imagistic style haunting, the comedy both physical and verbal, the contrapuntal sounds of gaiety and melancholy always present. Lesser stories of this same period lack this totality; sometimes their humor is forced, the story derivative, or the protagonist uninteresting.

The primary force in most of the "daylight" stories is memory. Paradoxically, memory unites delight and sadness. The narrator's pleasure in recalling days—even years—of joyous youth is heightened by his and the reader's nostalgia for lost innocence and the recognition of unfulfilled desires. Out of his memory Capote selects moments in time that catch the shimmer of sunlit childhood, in its brief happiness, its expectations and longings. He reminds us that all children dream a fairytale world, but all are

From *Truman Capote: A Study of the Short Fiction.* © 1992 by Twayne Publishers.

destined to awaken to painful reality. Although the stories differ in their plot particulars, their general outline is much the same: an event or an image triggers remembrance for the narrator, who then looks back to a childhood when everything seemed possible, and describes people from that period, friends, relatives, acquaintances. Eventually the person on whom the narrator focuses dies or goes away, and life thereafter is never the same.

"Children on Their Birthdays"

"Children on Their Birthdays," one of the earliest of Capote's published works, is a story both the author and the public favored. Miss Lily Jane Bobbit, the protagonist of the piece and a forerunner of the young woman in *Breakfast at Tiffany's*, is a 10-year-old girl who arrives in a small Alabama town with her mother one late summer afternoon. Although she lives in the community only a year, she has a powerful effect on everyone who knows her; Mr. C., the narrator of the story, declares that she will never be forgotten. Like a summer's day, Miss Bobbit's time is brief. The fact that she dies at the height of her hopes and desires, unspoiled by disappointments and failures, seems to make her ageless, untouched by process. Roses are in bloom the day of her death, and no leaves fall.

Though realistic enough in multiple ways, Lily Jane Bobbit is a fantasy child, the mirror of the longings of all children. The fantasy quality is suggested immediately upon her arrival. Although she gets off the six o'clock bus, it is as if she simply materializes from another world. We learn almost nothing about her past life. Like many a creature from other worlds, she is not destined to remain long in the world of ordinary mortals. She has no intentions of lingering to grow old in this sleepy Southern town, for she has plans to move on to Hollywood as soon as possible. She intends to be a star.

In the real world of children mothers (and fathers) exert control over their activities, but Lily Jane's mother does not interfere with anything Lily Jane does. Mrs. Bobbit has a speech defect and appears to be mute. In a role reversal that many a child might desire, Lily Jane seems to be in charge of her mother: "My mother has a disorder of the tongue, so it is necessary that I speak for her," the girl announces.[23] Further, the secret longing to be parentless and free to do whatever they want that children sometimes have is reinforced thematically by the absence of the father figure.[24] Although townspeople, church leaders, and school authorities try to control Lily Jane, nobody is able to direct her. She is what all children wish to be: free of parental restraint; free from attending school or church; free to criticize anything; free to make the friends she wants; free to earn money as she chooses and spend it as she prefers; free to do whatever she wants when she wants to do it. And, unlike a real child, who dreams impossible dreams but does nothing to achieve them, Miss Bobbit employs all her considerable energy to make her dreams reality.

She will not be diverted from her objectives in any way. From the moment of her arrival, when she interrupts Billy Bob's birthday party, everything she does is directed toward the fulfillment of her dream. However, this extraordinary child also has a practical side, the polar opposite of her romantic, dreamer side. She refuses to eat ice cream and cake because they are not good for the figure. The very night of her arrival, though she has good reason to rest after her long bus trip, she carries on with her dance practice. Although the adolescent boys fall in love with her, and the girls in their jealousy mock her, Miss Bobbit is indifferent to such behavior. Ordinary girls are silly and unkind, and ordinary boys are foolish and immature, but Lily Jane is practical, efficient, logical, and businesslike. She concentrates on her goal of achieving stardom. She will not go to school because it would be a waste of her time; school will not teach her what she needs to learn. Church too would be a waste of time, for God would be no use to her career plans. She needs the help of the devil, who is on her side, the side of dancing.

All the boys are happy to work on her behalf in any scheme she devises, but her one true friend is Rosealba, a black girl she rescued from the sexual bullying of these same white boys. Child-woman that Miss Bobbit is, a combination of innocence and worldliness, untouched by sexual stirrings and yet strangely knowing, she is totally different from all other girls. Undeterred by Billy Bob's mother, she gives Billy Bob a "refreshing" massage when he is ill; she rejects the boys' declaration of affection, but finds them entertaining; she shocks the local audience the night she wins the prize in a talent show when she sings a wicked little ditty and displays her blue-lacc-covered bottom.

Most of the humor in the story is associated with Miss Bobbit's personality and character, but Capote enlivens his tale with other kinds of humor that in time became Capote trademarks. There are funny scenes associated with animals: when Miss Bobbit is disturbed at night by the howling of dogs, she and Rosealba stalk the offenders. They carry "a flower basket filled with rocks; whenever they saw a dog they paused while Miss Bobbit scrutinized him. Sometimes she would shake her head, but more often she said, 'Yes, that's one of them, Sister Rosealba,' and Sister Rosealba, with ferocious aim, would take a rock from her basket and crack the dog between the eyes" ("Children," 98). The narrator notes that Miss Bobbit's landlady has a memorial sundial dedicated to a dog who met his end by lapping up paint. There is the comedy of exaggeration in the actions of the boys, particularly those of Preacher Star, who in spite of his name is the antithesis of a churchly child. There is the comedy of bizarrely inappropriate names. Rosealba Cat, for example, is neither a white rose nor a child of catlike grace—she is more like the "baby elephant" Mr. C. calls her. While Rosealba's name comically contradicts her appearance, Manny Fox's name emblemizes his personality. Fox is a sly con man so persuasive that a local woman gives him the money she had intended to use to buy an angel tombstone. Capote plays with language, as in the expression "Merci you kindly." Even food becomes a vehicle for fun; ordinary mortals eat boiled ham and deviled eggs, but Miss Bobbit will eat no meat, and only raw foods, including raw eggs. The humor of the tall tale, so popular with southern and western writers, and a device Capote employed frequently, appears here through such depictions as the old drunken boarder who has a toilet-paper phobia and the vengeance Miss Bobbit and Rosealba take on him for his behavior. Many of the girls' actions fall under the tall-tale category.

Capote gains maximum effect from humor, but the comedy, while very important to the story, is not the author's major concern. He always brings us back to the primary motif, the sweet and sad lost moments of childhood, days that can only be recaptured in idealized memory.

The imaginary and the nostalgic are brought together through the title, which comes from a statement made by Miss Bobbit, who is searching for a world where everything and everyone dances and is pretty, a special, lovely world "like children on their birthdays." Adults know that such a world does not exist, but Lily Jane is one of the creatures who lives in the sky, different from all others. She is the child who will never grow up. We have seen such a character in Oreilly, the clown who also lives in the sky, in "Master Misery," and that same metaphor is used later with Holly Golightly in *Breakfast at Tiffany's*. The child or childlike creature never remains with us for long. Oreilly disappears, Holly leaves forever, and Miss Bobbit dies.

Early or late, childhood and childhood's dreams fade. The images of William Blake's *Songs of Innocence* come to mind as we look at Capote's ephemeral characters: the children who want to continue playing are watched by adults who know how short the time is, who see the darkening green all around them. Experience must come, changing, shattering, completely destroying innocence and illusions. But this will not happen to Lily Jane Bobbit, who dies in her white communionlike dress, in summer, while the air is heavy with the fragrance of wisteria and roses, the rain soft against a rainbowed sky.

Also like Blake, Capote is a colorist, and throughout "Children on Their Birthdays" he makes yellow the major hue. Miss Bobbit is first seen in a lemon-colored dress; her eyes are the yellow of sunflowers; yellow roses are given to her in tribute, twice. The faces of the boys who bring her flowers look like "yellow moons." But the boys with their roses bring about Miss Bobbit's death as she runs toward them: "That is when the six o'clock bus ran over her" ("Children," 106). The yellow of flowers, of moons, of summer thus becomes associated with death in a gentle, melancholy, and nostalgic tone much like the one describing the yellow leaves of autumn Capote was to use in *The Grass Harp* and *Breakfast at Tiffany's*.[25]

The reader knows from the first that Miss Bobbit must die, for her death is announced by an opening line that has the same quiet finality as the conclusion: "Yesterday afternoon the six o'clock bus ran over Miss Bobbit." Death in general, and the death of Miss Bobbit in particular, is an inescapable fact for Capote and his readers. Even while spinning out the story with all its humor, the author uses delicate and transient images of summer, of mutable nature, to underscore the unalterable reality that the little girl will soon be gone, like the music heard from afar, the fireflies that swoop through the early evening, the brief blooming irises. Dressed in white and glitter soon after her arrival, the child is shown dancing just before the fall of darkness, illuminating the evening before night sets in. Fantasies, hopes, and dreams must end for those left behind, for those who must grow up. But the memory of summer and a magical child is caught and preserved forever.

THE GRASS HARP

The Grass Harp, a novella published in 1951, has many of the characteristics Capote favored in the forties, techniques seen in "Children on Their Birthdays," as well as in the 1958 novella *Breakfast at Tiffany's*, and as late as 1966, in *A Christmas Memory*. Although almost 20 years separate the earliest from the last of these four works, the stories not only seem part of a whole in multiple ways, but also fall into pairs: "Children on Their Birthdays" with *Breakfast at Tiffany's*, *The Grass Harp* with *A Christmas Memory*. All four have a young male narrator, easily identified with Capote; each has one or more major symbols that appear and reappear to bind the work together; the four feature recurring character types; each has a circular plot structure; all employ various forms of humor, from the very gentle to the physically vaudevillian; all create a sense of nostalgia for the past; in each, the most lasting impression is the combined sense of sadness and sweetness for the irretrievably lost world of childhood.

Capote turned *The Grass Harp* into a play a year after publication of the novella, but it was a failure with both the critics and the public. Although the novella is more effective than the play, the seeds of the play's failure are already present in the novella's overt message and its sentimentality; sentimentality exists in other Capote works, but he controls it more. He conveys the delicate, magical quality of memory quite successfully in the written words of the novella, but this key feature of the novella was lost when he embodied his story with characters and actions on stage.

The major symbol in *The Grass Harp* is the Indian grass found in the meadow just below the town cemetery. The grass harp, the narrator is informed by his cousin Dolly, is a teller of tales, and this is precisely the function the narrator takes on when he reaches manhood. He becomes the bard, like the harpist of ancient times. Introduced in the very first part of the story, the special grass is mentioned several times throughout the years that pass. The final revelation comes at the end when the narrator, still a boy and about to leave his home forever, goes with an elderly friend to visit the cemetery and the meadow below it, where the September grass glows in all its fall colors. As the two stand in the field, the narrator tells the old man of the ability of the grass to sing the stories of the lives of those who are now gone. At that moment we recognize the relationship of the grass and the human storyteller, as well as the circularity of the story. The story we read is the one the narrator himself tells, the one we have just heard, of a past he has relived through the retelling.

At the beginning of *The Grass Harp* the narrator suggests that everything that follows is filtered through memory. A segment of the past is revisited, but now, because it can never be relived and experienced as it actually was, it takes on new coloration and tone because the insignificant details of daily life are forgotten and meaningful episodes are highlighted. In language similar to that of several other Capote stories, the narrator reminds us that memory is selective. The narrator, Collin Fenwick, asks, "When was it ...?"[26] and a little later uses words like "long before." Soon he begins to tell us a story of "the lovely years" from the time of his arrival, an orphan, at age 11, to the day of his leavetaking, several years later.

After the death of his parents, Collin is taken in by his father's cousins, two spinsters, Verena and Dolly Talbo. Also living in the household is Dolly's dearest friend and constant companion, Catherine. Catherine is a dark-skinned woman who calls herself an indian, but the rest of the community call her a Negro and treat her as inferior. Dolly becomes Collin's closest ally and mentor, and he grows up in her and Catherine's constant company. Verena is the money-maker, the businesswoman of the family, whose greed and selfishness lead to the death of her sister, Dolly, and to the end of Collin's innocence.

Before Dolly's death, however, life follows a quiet, predictable pattern. Dolly is as much a child as Collin. She likes children's play and games, has the pink room of a little girl, and prefers sweets to any other food. She does not have to pretend to enter into the childhood stage Collin is in, for she seems to have been always caught there. Only in the last few months of her life does she become an independent, self-assured woman.

Dolly makes, and sells a tonic to alleviate dropsy. Similar to the format of the later story, *A Christmas Memory*, with its seasonal trips into the woods to collect the ingredients for fruitcake, *The Grass Harp* presents making the dropsy medicine as the focal point of the week for Dolly, Catherine, and Collin. On Saturdays they take to the woods to search out the herbs, the roots, the bark, and the leaves that go into the secret remedy. Because of the sales of her medicine, Dolly has contact through the mail with customers outside her immediate circle. These letters are her only connection with other people because she is shy and timid. The money she earns from the sales provides the three companions with games, puzzles, lessons, and whatever advertised items catch their fancy.

This happy time ends when Collin is 16. Verena decides that real money can be made from the production and sale of the medicine. Verena, unable to allow her sister anything of her own, brings in an adviser from Chicago, which, in the xenophobic South of those years, represents sin city.[27] The townspeople tag Dr. Morris Ritz as a foreigner and a troublemaker, and they are right. With Ritz's advice, Verena prepares to go into large-scale production of the dropsy cure. But the plan never comes to fruition because Dolly refuses to yield to Verena.

Ritz is a con man drawn in the mold of the earlier Manny Fox, from "Children on Their Birthdays."[28] Both are sly and manipulative. Fox is "greasy and leering" as he tells off-color jokes; Ritz winks suggestively as he speaks to Collin of sexual opportunities in Chicago. Fox, the vaudeville showmaster, claps his hands; Dr. Ritz, of unknown profession, snaps his fingers as if he were in a vaudeville show. The townspeople's suspicions, Dolly's fears, and Catherine's hostility to Ritz prove well-founded, for Ritz eventually takes off with Verena's money and leaves her a broken, disappointed woman.

The turning point in the story occurs on the night Verena forces a showdown with Dolly about the dropsy cure. Not only does Verena berate her; she also blames her for the lonely life she has been forced to live because she has been ashamed of Dolly and the "gurgling fool," Catherine. Now Dolly feels she can no longer live with her sister. Although Verena tells her she has no other place to go, Dolly leaves home. Dolly, joined by Catherine and Collin, walks through the sleeping town; together they pass through the Indian grass, the grass that is the harp. As the sun rises they reach the China tree where they will live until the beginning of October.

Although the first part of the novella has a childlike, magical quality, the second segment, which describes life in the treehouse, is even closer to a fairy tale, but one with strong didactic elements. Here, Dolly and Collin grow up, with Dolly discovering her strength of character as well as her womanhood. They find friendships, and they and some of the people who become their friends learn about love. Typical of a fairy tale, they must undergo a test and be physically and emotionally challenged by various forces.

When Dolly, Catherine, and Collin take up life in the treehouse—surely the dream of many a child—they find happiness for a short time. Many people seek them out. A young man, Riley Henderson, and an old man, Judge Cool, join them as allies in the ensuing battles between the forces of conservatism and the forces of change. The handsome daredevil Riley becomes Collin's much admired friend; Judge Cool and Dolly fall in love. Each fulfills the needs of the other. For Dolly, the Judge becomes the admirer she has never had, one who approves of all she is and accepts her totally. For the Judge, Dolly becomes the beloved to whom all may be told.

The people in the treehouse learn lessons, about the world, about other people, and about the self. Uncertain men change to lovers and heroes. In old age, Dolly comes of age, becomes a woman who stands tall and assured because of love. But the treedwellers also learn that there is no escape from responsibilities. Eventually each must return to face the issues and problems he or she left behind. Dolly chooses to go back to her sister, who needs her. The Judge must also resolve his family problems. Riley will no longer behave like an irresponsible, uncontrollable boy, and Collin will move toward self-sufficient manhood.

The story's underlying didacticism is mitigated by the liveliness of Capote's humor. The humor in the first part is more gentle, more verbal than that in the second: Catherine abandons French lessons after she learns how to say she is tired in French, for example, and she invents a version of history that suits her theories of race. The comedy of the second segment involves mock battle scenes and numerous farcical characters, some of whose names identify their personalities. Most of the interlopers suggest Gilbert and

Sullivan figures. Capote mocks traditional religious figures and their attitudes, not only through their behavior, but also by creating a highly comic and sympathetic evangelist named Sister Ida Honey, who has an enormous brood of children, most of them illegitimate, but all loved. The tall-tale element is prevalent throughout this part of the story, as when Sister Ida recounts her various romances and ensuing pregnancies, or a meal intended for 5 is expanded to serve 16, or in the manner by which the good defeat the wicked invaders.

Comedic episodes dominate the middle section of the story, but the reader is never allowed to forget that nothing good lasts. With the departure of most of the people at the end of the battle, decisions about the future must be made. Dolly cannot resist Verena's pleas to return home. Just as Verena's claim seems to stand between Dolly and a new life, so too does the season, with its melancholy turn in the weather. As Dolly hesitates, attempting to choose, the rain seems to separate her from the Judge. The rain here, like the rain described as a curtain of glass in "The Headless Hawk," suggests a barrier that cannot be breeched. With the rain also comes the dissolution of cozy living in the treehouse. Everything falls, spills, or is washed away. The group leaves and takes nothing with them. What remains will be covered over by winter.

The warning of the winter to come has been present from the moment Dolly decided to leave home. From that point on in the story, the reader has a growing awareness of the swift passage of time. Before Dolly even tells Collin of her plans to go live in the treehouse with Catherine, Collin is lying in bed thinking of dead fathers—Dolly's and his own—and of the Indian grass and its stories of the dead. As Dolly agrees to permit Collin to join her in flight, a clock tolls the hour. Even in the idyllic setting of the treehouse, the Judge's gold watch is often mentioned, ticking away; although Dolly, in a magnanimous gesture, gives the watch to Sister Ida to help her and her children on their journey, time cannot be stopped. The clock is running down for Dolly, who becomes ill soon after returning home. The night of her death, just before she goes up to the attic with Collin in search of some decorations, he becomes aware of the striking of the town clock. Later, as she shows him her childhood treasures, Collin describes her face as looking like a moth's next to a lamp, so delicate is she, so brief her remaining time. Before the clock strikes again, Dolly tells Collin of the important knowledge she has gained from the Judge: "love is a chain of love.... Because when you can love one thing ... you can love another, and that is owning, that is something to live with" (*Grass Harp*, 223).

Soon the sound of the clock is heard again. Moments afterward, as Dolly is dancing around the attic, she collapses. Her death at sunrise is known to Collin even before he is told, for a breeze flutters through the veil of Dolly's traveling hat, the hat she wore when they left for the treehouse, in River Woods, near the cemetery and the meadow of Indian grass. Although Dolly's death is really the end of the story, the aftermath of the lives of her friends and family are briefly summarized. Everything and everyone changes when she is gone. For Collin, childhood and the lovely years are over; he leaves home with no expectation of ever returning again.

BREAKFAST AT TIFFANY'S

From the day of its publication in 1958 *Breakfast at Tiffany's* has been a much-loved book. More than 30 years after its appearance, book reviewers continue to compare female characters to Holly Golightly, Capote's unforgettable heroine.

Numerous conflicting stories have been told about the model for Capote's portrait. An actual person sparked the fictional creation, but who that person was remains a topic of debate. Typically, Capote embroidered and embellished the truth, telling different versions of the origin of Holly Golightly to interviewers over the years, and also to his biographer. All of these statements are at odds with novelist James Michener's recollections of the original "starlet-singer-actress-raconteur" he knew to be Holly.[29]

Although an actual person may have provided the mold for the heroine, Holly is yet another fantasy creature, a beautiful, captivating, elusive, lovable, and haunting young woman, a mixture of the romantic and the tragic. Generally regarded by critics as an expanded, older version of the adolescent Lily Jane Bobbit of "Children on Their Birthdays," Holly has many of the same personality traits: wisdom beyond her chronological age, brashness, courage, a longing for something that proves unattainable, and a separateness which makes her different from earthbound human beings. We respond affectionately to both Lily Jane and Holly, laughing at and with them, and mourning their loss. However, because *Breakfast at Tiffany's* is the longer, more complex fiction in which the major character is more fully drawn, the minor characters funnier, and the setting more completely realized, it is the more memorable work.

Mr. C., the narrator of "Children," has an expanded role in the novella. Though he has no name except the one Holly gives him briefly, he is obviously meant to be the young Capote, starting out as a writer in New

York; even the birthdays are the same, September 30.[30] In *Breakfast at Tiffany's*, however, the Capote figure is more than an observer. He is an involved participant who falls in love with Holly and helps her whenever she has problems. He is friend, listener, defender, brother, and ultimately biographer of this captivating creature.

This story, resembling other Capote pieces in its mixture of tenderness, melancholy, and humor, is enclosed and protected in a frame of memory, inviolable, like figures carved on an urn, caught in a moment of time past. As in many of Capote's stories, time is the silent yet relentless figure in the background. In reality, autumn and winter must eventually succeed spring and summer; the church clock must toll the hours, signifying the passage of time and time-bound life. But memory, misted over with all its happy and unhappy moments, remains. The narrator's recollections are stirred by a phone call and a visit to a barman named Joe Bell. Returning to a neighborhood he knew well 15 years earlier, he learns that Joe has obtained a recent photo of a sculpted African head and that this head bears an uncanny resemblance to a much-loved person out of the past, Holly Golightly. After the bartender relates what little information he has concerning the background of the photo, the narrator walks through the neighborhood streets, back to the brownstone where he first met Holly.

It was wartime when the hopeful young writer met Holly, who lived in the same building as he. Holly, not quite 19, was a young woman who lived on "powder room money," a girl who looked like a breakfast cereal ad, but lived solely for fun and excitement. The larky atmosphere, the casual encounters, the easy money, the nightclubs, the dancing in the streets and partying with service officers—all speak of a wartime philosophy. The whole world seems young. Champagne bubbles up in glasses, in spite of or because of the war, but the war is very far away, even for Holly, whose beloved brother is at the front. When he is killed, however, her one tie with the past and normal life is destroyed.

Holly's card vaguely identifies her occupation as "traveling." The word is apt for the way she lives. Holly never stays anywhere for very long. She is a person searching for love, for a home, for a happy and safe life—all symbolized in her mind by Tiffany's. Orphaned early, the then Lulamae Barnes married Doc Golightly when she was only a child. Although she loves him—he was like a kind old father to her—she ran away. From that moment she has had a series of fantasy lives. In Hollywood, where for a time she concentrated on improving herself, Lulamae became Holly; she lost her hillbilly accent, learned a little French, became a starlet, and gained enough sophistication to realize she could not become a star. She then headed for New York to try for another kind of fame and fortune as a New York socialite. The elusive Holly is depicted as someone balanced between childhood and womanhood. In spite of her numerous lovers, she appears untouched by sordidness, and is surprisingly naive in many ways. Having had no childhood, she creates a child's world where she makes up the rules. Her girlish enthusiasm is contagious, so that all men feel more alive in her company.

In New York, although fortune eludes her, she does find fame, that is, notoriety, when she unwittingly becomes a courier for a mobster named Sally Tomato. This experience ends her only "non-rat" romance, when her skittish lover abandons her. The publicity also causes her to flee the country to avoid the courts and keep from betraying Sally, for she is an advocate of the honest heart in all circumstances. The streetwise side of Holly recognizes that her "career" in New York has been blemished and part of her life is over. Because of this mishap, once again Holly becomes a traveler. After sending a single postcard to the narrator, she fades into the soft haze of the past, a past revisited briefly when Joe Bell sends for the narrator.

All of Holly's fantasizing has a melancholy side, however, for it is really only a dream. Beneath the surface of gaiety lies the knowledge that nothing lasts. There is loneliness at the core of the dreamer. Though always surrounded by people, Holly gives the impression of being alone, still the little girl, Lulamae Barnes, still running, still searching for a home never to be hers. She knows she is one of those wild creatures who live in the sky, always an empty place; her favorite song tells plaintively of traveling "through the pastures of the sky." At times Holly confesses to the narrator her awareness of transiency, and in a sorrowful moment of revelation tells him we do not even recognize the wonder of lovely days until they are gone. Then it is too late to bring them back. For the narrator, however, they can be recalled, though only in memory.

Holly may seem like Miss Bobbit in her unchanging hope for something better, something more, but there is a far greater strain of melancholy in Holly. Holly, unlike Miss Bobbit, seems to know, at least at a subliminal level, that life will never give what it seems to promise children. Miss Bobbit dies before knowledge dims her radiance. Holly, however, even as a child, never had the kind of innocence Lily Jane has. There is a depth of sadness in her unknown to the younger girl. In spite of Holly's determination to be happy and have everything possible, she has been battered by existence and has endured poverty, hunger, loss, and abandonment.

An authority on abandonment, Holly has learned to face the world with style, even if it is veneer. When the narrator tries to tell her gently about the defection of her lover, Jose, Holly first puts on her makeup, her perfume, her earrings, and her dark glasses before she reads Jose's letter, in which he informs her that he will not marry her. A young woman who has built her personality partly on dissemblance and make-believe, partly playful, partly defensive, Holly has her own kind of armor to protect her from the harsh world. This is what leads her former Hollywood agent, O. J. Berman, to call her "a phony," but also to note that "She isn't a phony because she is a *real* phony. She believes all this crap she believes."[31]

Berman also predicts that Holly one day will finish "at the bottom of a bottle of Seconals." Although Holly battles frequently with fear and depression, in the tenderness of the narrator's memory, however, she is always young and unchanged. Still, the images associated with Holly lend themselves to both visions, Berman's and the narrator's: a birdcage she presents to the young writer, given with the admonition that he must never put anything in it; the cast-off cat she takes in, refuses to name, and then abandons when she flees New York; the yellow roses she loves (reminding the reader of the death of Miss Bobbit in "Children on Their Birthdays"); the flowers Joe Bell attempts to give her when she is leaving, flowers that fall to the floor (again reminiscent of the flowers Miss Bobbit never gets in the last scene in the short story). The downpour of rain as Holly flees New York carries with it the wind of desolation, an ache not obviated when the narrator discovers the cat at a later time ensconced in a lace-curtained window in Harlem. He hopes then that Holly too will find a place where she belongs, but that hope, the reader recognizes, may be as ephemeral as her promise to keep in touch.

Although both the short story and the novella end with a sense of loss in their images of mist and rain, a much more powerful minor key runs through the conclusion of the later work, for summer is still in the air in "Children on Their Birthdays." The rainbow that crosses the sky preserves the feeling of childlike hope, but in *Breakfast at Tiffany's* the autumnal season of heavy rain and yellowed leaves suggests only the winter to come.

However, *Breakfast at Tiffany's*, like "Children on Their Birthdays," is also lighthearted in many ways. Once again, Capote's humor is found in characters, dialogue, and events. He plays with names: Joe Bell takes phone messages; Rusty Trawler is a much-married man who has been involved in sex scandals.[32] Runyonesque characters from New York and Hollywood fill the novella. There is a chase scene with horses. And the star of the story herself provides slapstick and bawdy humor. *Breakfast at Tiffany's* shows Capote at his best, in total control as humorist, stylist, symbolist, imagist, and tone painter, characteristics that marked his fiction and nonfiction prose of the fifties and sixties.

Notes

23. "Children on Their Birthdays," in *A Capote Reader*, 93; hereafter cited in text as "Children."

24. There is an autobiographical element here, in that the author's family life was somewhat like Miss Bobbit's: her mother is mute, and her father is absent, and Capote grew up without mother or father.

25. Capote associates the color green with death, and usually combines green with gothic images of horror, terror, or violence. Capote also associates the color yellow with death, but links this color with nostalgia or sadness.

26. *The Grass Harp in A Capote Reader*, 155; hereafter cited in text.

27. The southern parallel, at least as described in faulkner's novels, is Memphis.

28. Although Manny Fox in "Children on Their Birthdays," is not called a Jew, this identity is suggested. Dr. Ritz is often refferred to as the "little Jew," usually by the Catherine, who is an outspoken woman. She says things others are too polite or kind to voice.

29. See Michener's "Foreword" in Lawrence Grobe's *Conversations with Capote* (New York: New American Library, 1985).

30. Capote also makes an oblique reference to another autobiographical detail, when he speaks of being fired for "an amusing misdemeanor." He is probably referring to the Robert Frost episode at *the New Yorker*. See Helen S. Garson's *Truman Capote* and Gerald Clarke's *Capote: A Biography*.

31. *Breakfast at Tiffany's*, in *A Capote Reader*, 241–242; hereafter cited in text as *Breakfast*.

32. The names Lily Jane in "Children on Their Birthdays" and Lulamae in *Breakfast at Tiffany's* appear to have a relationship to the author's mother, whose name was Lillie Mae before she changed it to Nina.

BRIAN CONNIFF

"Psychological Accidents": In Cold Blood and Ritual Sacrifice

Amerian prison literature of the past twenty-five years has been preoccupied with a contradiction that is central to the national consciousness. Throughout this period, imprisonment and execution have often risen to the level of obsession; yet such authorized violence has been so normalized that any understanding of it, even in the relatively "safe" realm of literature, has rarely occurred, except through personal tragedy or accident. It is hard to imagine that even Malcolm X, whose *Autobiography* H. Bruce Franklin considers the starting point of "Contemporary American prison literature" (236), would ever have considered the institutionalized racism of the justice system if he had remained a petty hustler in Detroit. As Malcolm himself explains, it took a ten-year sentence for a first-time burglary conviction—a sentence lengthened by the involvement of two "well-to-do" white women—to begin his transformation from an ordinary con into the leading disciple of Elijah Muhammad, and then into a symbol of the "aspirations" held by those convicts of the late 1960s and early 1970s who wanted, as Eldridge Cleaver puts it, to "inject" the problems of imprisonment "into national and state politics" (59, 61). It is equally hard to imagine that Cleaver himself could ever have been transformed from a harmless "lover of marijuana" into an "insurrectionary" rapist, and then into a leading Black Panther, if he had not had the bad luck to serve a term in San

From *The Midwest Quarterly* 35 (Autumn 1995). © 1993 by Pittsburg State University.

Quentin on a petty charge of possession. It might very well have taken the chance correspondence with Jack Henry Abbott to allow Norman Mailer, in the course of writing *The Executioner's Song*, to see through his usual glamorizations of violence, from the 1950s hipster to Mike Tyson, into the reality of the institutionalized man, and beyond that into what he would call, in his introduction to Abbott's *In the Belly of the Beast*, "the progressive institutionalization of all society" (xv). Again and again, this literature of the prison suggests that the most fortified barriers are not the physical walls and fences between the prison, and the outside world; the most fortified barriers are the psychological walls between the preoccupations of everyday life, even the everyday life of a petty hustler or a famous novelist, and the conscious realization that punishment is the most self-destructive kind of national addiction.

Ironically, these psychological walls are confronted most forcefully, and their implications are seen most clearly, in a work that is not usually considered hard-core enough, or subversive enough, to be a part of any renegade tradition of "prison literature": Truman Capote's *In Cold Blood*. In the novel's most characteristic moment, Kansas Bureau of Investigation Agent Alvin Dewey—one of Capote's favorite "characters"—finally hears the confession of Perry Smith, one of the two former Kansas State Penetentiary cellmates who murdered Herb Clutter, a prosperous farmer, and his family. For seven months, Dewey has worked continuously, staring at grisly photos and following useless leads, in his quest "to learn 'exactly what happened in that house that night.'" But when he finally hears the entire story—told by one of the killers, step by step, shotgun blast by shotgun blast—he is strangely disappointed. The truth, he discovers, is even more disturbing than anything he had imagined. Even though he suddenly knows more about the crime than he, or Capote, would ever have hoped, the "true story" somehow "fails to satisfy his sense of meaningful design" (277). The truth, Dewey discovers, is at once more ordinary and more disturbing than anything he has been able to imagine. Contrary to his expectations, Smith and Richard Hickock did not kill the Clutters out of some aberrant sense of revenge; in fact, until the night of the crime, they had never even met their chosen victims. They certainly were not, in any sense, "criminal masterminds." In fact, they were not even very competent. Among other things, they had never even bothered to find out what everyone else in town seemed to know, that Herb Clutter never kept more than a few dollars on hand. Perhaps most disturbing of all, they acted as though they were simply putting in a rather ordinary night's work for which they believed they deserved a good night's pay—though, as it turned out, they would come away with nothing more than about forty dollars and a radio. To Agent Dewey, hearing the full story for the first time, none of this seems possible. He does not want to consider the obvious truth, that "The crime was a psychological accident, virtually an impersonal act; the victims might as well have been struck by lightning" (277).

Like the works more often recognized as "prison literature," *In Cold Blood* is primarily concerned with moments like these, in which "meaningful designs" about crime and punishment—the kind of "common sense" virtually no one sees fit to question—are disrupted by actual events. But no matter how accidental or incongruous the Clutter murders might have seemed, Capote went to Kansas with a "meaningful design" of his own, one far more serious than the literary establishment, the popular imagination, or he himself would later admit. As Gerald Clarke has written in his recent biography, Capote would tell just about anyone who happened to listen that he planned to examine "the reaction of a small town to a hideous crime" (324). For such a study, he did not believe that the solution of the crime was particularly relevant—a belief that angered Alvin Dewey, and would undoubtedly have angered most local residents, if they had been willing, at that early stage, to take him seriously. Capote was not the least bit concerned with the killers, at first, but only with the immediate victims—a category in which he included both the Clutter family and their neighbors, all those people who suddenly found their lives altered by the mere proximity of the slain bodies.

But Capote's understanding of this "reaction" was, at first, severely limited: to suppose that the effects of violence do not include the capture and punishment of the criminals is to underestimate the community's need for retribution, its need to reaffirm its "stability," its "normalcy," by authorizing and enacting a violence of its own. Capote also underestimated the extent to which he, too, was subject to the irresistable force of this need. He seems to have never been able to admit—or perhaps even understand—just how much the "appearance" of Hickock and Smith, in both senses of the word, caused him to alter, and eventually fictionalize, his "nonfiction novel."

When the good citizens of Holcomb and Garden City finally decided to talk to Capote, he found, or at least he imagined he found, the reaction he had anticipated: locked doors and sleepless nights, suspicious neighbors and frightened children, malicious gossip and charitable prayers. Accordingly, the first half of *In Cold Blood* is filled with this superficial fear, which Capote typically describes as a nostalgia for an "ordinary" life—as though he is not yet aware, or will not yet allow his narrative voice to sound aware, of the forces that lie behind this "normalcy." After all, as Capote writes, these people had always been "quite content to exist inside ordinary life." They had been reasonably happy, it seems, "to work, to hunt, to watch television, to attend school socials, choir practice, meetings of the 4-H Club." In fact, as the most banal cliché would have it, they had been "sufficiently unfearful of each other to seldom trouble to lock their doors" (15).

Once this "unfearful" life was corrupted by the Clutter murders, it could not be restored until after the killers had been found and punished. Finally compelled to lock their doors, many of them with newly purchased locks, the local residents seemed at first to be trying to keep out some kind of invader from "outside" the community, some kind of creature as alien as it was frightening. They seemed to be playing the kind of game that Agent Dewey, searching one more time through the photographs of the crime scene in the hope that "some meaningful detail would declare itself," described as "find the hidden animals" (100). As George Creeger has noted, Dewey's search for "animals" in the "puzzle" is part of an elaborate system of imagery that Capote uses "to suggest a complex relationship between the criminal and the community" (6). The "grim logic" by which Hickock and Smith are categorized as "animals" allows the community to "deprive the killers of their humanity," "exile them" and "return to the feeling it cherishes so much—that of security" (2, 6). But Capote also suggests that Dewey's search through the "puzzle" is also a little naive, almost even pathetic: it is a child's game, in relation to the events that have preceded it, and the events that will follow. "Meaning" will never declare itself. Rather, "meaning" will have to be superimposed, over and over, by all the residents of Garden City, and eventually by Capote himself, as one delusion after another is undermined by ordinary, sordid events.

Because a common "normalcy" ultimately depends upon the complete exclusion of "outsiders," the exorcism of these mysterious "animals" is just as important as their discovery and capture. In this sense, most of Holcomb's citizens are very much like Perry Smith's sister, who believes that men like Perry and his father—the Irish rodeo cowboy turned wilderness man, John "Tex" Smith—"should" always live "alone," perhaps in the "Alaskan wilderness," far away from her own kind of "timid life" (153, 209). Like all the rest of the "normals," as Perry calls them—"respectable people, safe and smug people"—she needs to convince herself that Perry's life is "an ugly and lonely progress toward one mirage and then another" (277). In other words, she needs to believe that Perry's life is completely different from her own, and completely different from the lives of those other "respectable" people with whom she tries to surround herself. Only Perry and his kind, beasts from some imagined "wilderness," could so disrupt and endanger a community in which lives are assumed to have direction—a world of progress that is always becoming, as Herb Clutter confidently remarked in an interview with C. B. Palmer not long before his death, "increasingly organized" (6). Like the residents of Holcomb, Perry's sister must convince herself that it is only people like Perry, "isolated" and "animal," who are driven by a lonely search for distant "mirages."

As the local "professional," Agent Dewey assumes the responsibility of superimposing on the evidence an official interpretation that can somehow support these delusions. Accordingly, in his efforts to explain the crime, he constructs two "concepts." Dewey realizes that both have glaring limitations, and he has difficulty deciding between them; nonetheless, these "concepts," and Dewey's inclinations in trying to decide, allow Capote to provide a commentary on the kind of respectability to which Perry's sister, like so many others, has always aspired. According to the first possible explanation, the "single killer concept," the killer would have been "a friend of the family, or, at any rate, a man with more than casual knowledge of the house and its inhabitants." This person would have known the structure of the house, the placing of the telephones, the dog's fear of guns and, of course, "that the doors were seldom locked" (98). Dewey is reluctant to accept this explanation, because it would lead him to assume elaborate and careful planning on the part of this "single killer." The killer would have had to possess the kind of rationality that, Dewey would rather believe, distinguishes people like those of his community from animals and madmen. The second "concept" follows the first "in many essentials," but suggests that the killer had an "accomplice, who helped subdue the family, tape, and time them" (99). Dewey is even more reluctant to accept this second explanation—though of course it turns out to be closer to the truth. He finds it "difficult to understand 'how two individuals could reach the same degree of rage, the kind of psychopathic rage it took to commit such a crime'" (99). "Psychopathic rage" is the one idea he could not have derived from the "facts" in which he claims to place so much faith. For that matter, this idea even allows him to deny an impressive body of evidence—the mattress box placed beneath Herb Clutter's body, the pillow beneath his son's head, the blankets tucked around the two women—all the traces of "considerate impulses ... a certain twisted tenderness" on the part of at least one killer (122). Nonetheless, Dewey clings to this second "concept" as long as he can, because in the common scheme of things, which he wants so badly to reaffirm, the very definition of the "psychopathic" would be the murder of people like the Clutters, the embodiments of local respectability, the "least likely people in the world" to be killed (102).

Dewey's two "concepts" are revealing not only because of the extent to which they exclude the reality of the crime, but also because of the extent to which they exclude each other: he does not want to admit the possibility of either a calculated, multiple murder or the possibility of mutual psychopathology. Most of all, he does not want to admit the possibility of *both*, that two killers, together, could have performed such a crime, deliberately and without "abnormal" rage—as, in fact, they did. As a professional defender of the community—and as a defender of the very idea of a "community" by which rational "normalcy" is defined—he must always view "psychopathology" as individual. He must always believe that rational deliberation necessarily excludes excessive violence, except as they might come together within a narrowly defined category of individual psychopathology. At the same time, as a custodian of the law, he must neatly divide all offenders "into two groups, the 'sane' and the 'insane'" (335). Most basically, like Perry Smith's sister, and like most everyone else in Holcomb, Dewey wants desperately to believe that the Clutter murders were the act of someone completely isolated, mentally *and* socially.

Dewey's theories might have remained impressive, like Capote's original plan for his book, and almost convincing, if it were not for the intervention of certain "accidents." By a stroke of luck far more striking than Capote's "discovery" of the story, the crime is "solved." In the Kansas State Penitentiary, Floyd Wells, a former cellmate of Richard Hickock, happens to hear a radio account of the murder. Wanting, more than anything else, to improve his own chances of parole, Wells decides to inform the prison officials. In the meantime, by returning to their favorite motels and continuing to pass bad checks, Smith and Hickock have just about guaranteed their own arrest outside a Las Vegas post office. Capote's narrative arrangement—more or less alternating scenes involving the Clutters and their community with scenes involving Smith and Hickock—provides the kind of juxtapositions that make the murderers' simple incompetence all the more glaring, in contrast to the elaborate suspicions and theories fostered by the "normal" community.

By virtue of such unimpressive events, Capote found himself in a situation that would turn out to be far more resistant to his investigations and his art than the reticence of Kansas farmers. Perhaps it was only such events, combined with the trial and execution that would follow—in which "good" would stubbornly refuse to triumph over "evil," in which "sanity" would strangely refuse to explain and cure "insanity"—that could ever have forced him to question his initial design. Perhaps it was only such events that could have allowed him to travel—by such an unexpected route and, in the end, deeper than he had ever anticipated—into the center of the American psyche. In any case, when word got around that the killers were being brought back for trial, Capote made sure that he was at the center of the crowd forming outside the Finney County Court House to await their arrival. There, journalists anticipated "shouted abuse." Just about everyone, anxious for the display of the "hidden animals," anticipated some kind of worthwhile spectacle. But the moment the killers appeared, this design, too, was shattered. At the sight of Smith and Hickock, everyone simply fell silent, "as though amazed to find them humanly shaped" (280).

This amazement at the sight of the killers is a clue to the "effect of fear" that is, of all the effects the novel tries to document, the most resistant to conscious awareness. The capture of Smith and Hickock is not enough, in itself, to make the residents of Holcomb feel completely secure. And the public display of the two killers—"white-faced and blinking blindly" as they "glistened in the glare of flashbulbs and floodlights" (280)—only serves to undermine whatever small degree of security has been restored. In fact, Capote suggests, the combination of these two events only exposes a deeper hostility—a hostility within the community for which the two murderers cannot be completely responsible. The demonization of these "Persons Unknown" turns out to have been, all along, a defense against the very nightmare that does come true the moment they are put on show in the courthouse square: the killers, as it turns out, are not so reassuringly "alien." With the arrest of Smith and Hickock, the residents of Holcomb have been spared what might have seemed, at first, to be a worse "solution" of the crime, the possibility that the killers might be found "among themselves." So, now, one might expect them to be relieved that they no longer have "to endure the unique experience of distrusting each other" (105), at least not in exactly the same way.

But even though it has turned out that Smith and Hickock are not "locals," for some reason their appearance can not extinguish "the fires of mistrust in the glare of which many old neighbors viewed each other strangely, and as strangers" (15). Even when Hickock's detailed confession is announced—as though any further evidence is needed—the people of Holcomb still want to believe that someone else, someone more familiar, must have been involved: "the majority of Holcomb's population, having lived for seven weeks amid unwholesome rumors, general mistrust, and suspicion, appeared to feel disappointed at being told that the murderer was not someone among themselves" (262). They cannot escape the kind of internal distrust that was first expressed by Myrtle Clare, postmistress and local Jeremiah, immediately after the murders. As Mrs. Clare told her mother, it could have been anyone: "All the neighbors are rattlesnakes. Varmints looking for a chance to slam the door in your face. It's the same the world over" (85). Ironically, it is only after the killers have been caught and returned to Kansas that Mrs. Clare's vast denunciation begins to acquire a degree of general acceptance. No matter how vigorously the citizens have taken to buying new locks and to constructing psychological theories, they are still compelled to confront a beast that is within. Just as "Institutional dourness and cheerful domesticity coexist on the fourth floor of the Finney County Courthouse," where Smith and Hickock wait for their trial, institutionalized fear and domestic ritual remain inseparable in the minds of all the people who wait to see them tried (283). The arrest and display of the killers is not enough, at least not so long as they refuse to appear obviously inhuman. The community still cannot return to "normal," not until the fear and the ritual are completely fused in another act of violence.

That is why the good citizens of Finney County finally seem to be seeking—at once and, ultimately, in defiance of all evidence—a criminal without *and* a criminal within, a guilty alien *and* a guilty neighbor. Though Capote is never quite willing to pursue all of its implications, he does suggest that such a paradox is inevitably involved in the dynamics of ritual sacrifice. As René Girard explains, in *Violence and the Sacred*, the victim "must bear a sharp resemblance to the *human* categories excluded from the ranks of the sacrificable, while still maintaining a degree of difference that forbids all possible confusion" (12). To mitigate internal distrust—or even better, to pretend that it has never existed—the community must seize upon a "sacrificable" victim, or, in the case of *In Cold Blood*, victims. Otherwise, the community fears, further violence might "be vented on its own members, the people it most desires to protect" (4). Accordingly, everyone in town has demonized Hickock and Smith, turned them into "animals," in order to insist, as Girard puts it, on a "degree of difference that avoids all confusion"; and, more by chance than anything else, it has discovered the killers to be all too human—more or less ordinary looking young men, without elaborate criminal records. The killers turn out to be too a little close to "the *human* catagories excluded from the ranks of the sacrificable."

Capote's depiction of the murder trial is, in effect, an attempt to demonstrate that this contradiction can only be overcome—and Hickock and Smith properly executed—if their actual mental states are treated as irrelevant. No legal consideration can be given to the car collision that left Dick Hickock, in his father's words, no longer "the same boy" (191), nor to the first seventeen months he did in the state prison at Lansing for taking a hunting knife from a neighbor's house. As Hickock's father puts it, this first imprisonment seems, more than anything else, to have been the young man's "ruination": "When he came out of Lansing, he was a total stranger to me" (191). Nor can any legal consideration be given to Smith's "personality structure," described by one psychiatrist as "very nearly that of a paranoid schizophrenic reaction" (43, 333-34). Certainly, it is necessary to exclude from the trial Smith's recurrent dream of an avenging yellow parrot, a "towering" figure that first visited him when he was a child in a California orphanage run by nuns who beat and humiliated him for wetting the bed, the "warrior-angel" that came to his rescue and "blinded the nuns with its beak, fed upon their eyes, slaughtered them as they 'pleaded for mercy,' then so gently lifted him, enfolded him, winged him away to paradise"—a magic friend that reappeared violently throughout his "several confinements in institutions and children's detention centers" (109, 111).

In this way, Copote suggests, the community reassures itself that justice is being carried out, while establishing the adequacy of the sacrificable victims. To this end, the prosecution of Smith and Hickock is aided by the M'Naghten rule, "the ancient British importation which contends that if the accused knew the nature of his act, and knew it was wrong, then he is mentally competent and responsible for his actions" (301). "Furthermore," as special assistant prosecuting attorney Logan Green reminds the Judge, there is "nothing in the Kansas statutes indicating that the physicians chosen to determine a defendant's mental condition must be of any particular qualification." They can be "just plain doctors. Medical doctors in general practice. That's all the law requires" (301). Like the two "concepts" superimposed on the case by Agent Dewey before the killers were captured, the Kansas statutes serve the community's purpose, in this case by reducing psychiatric testimony, literally, to a "yes" or "no" answer, preferably given by an "expert" who would not even be disposed, in any case, to much further elaboration. Despite the public and the media's earlier fascination with the capture and confessions of the killers, no attempt is made, once they are caught, to understand the crime in any way. Rather, as the execution of Hickock and Smith draws closer, the most troubling questions are systematically preempted. Neither the community nor the law that defends it—and, in the end, not even Capote himself, the aspiring expert on "multiple murderers"—really wants to risk any challenge to the accepted distinctions between the "sacrificable victims," Hickock and Smith, and all those local residents who must be "excluded from the ranks of the sacrificable." As one of the forensic psychiatrists asked to consult on the evaluations of the two killers admits, in the kind of testimony excluded from the trial, "murderers who seem rational, coherent, and controlled, and yet whose homicidal acts have a bizarre, apparently senseless quality, pose a difficult problem" (335).

Capote is admirably determined to confront this kind of difficult problem, mostly by including in the novel the kind of testimony that is excluded with such vigilance from the courtroom. Throughout, he dwells on the dual nature of the sacrificial victim. Early on, he describes Hickock's face, transformed by a car collision into a jumble of "mismatched parts," part "American-style 'good kid,'" part thug. Smith's body is similarly "mismatched," the result of a motor-cycle accident that left his weight-lifter's upper-body balanced tenuously on two "dwarfish" legs, which "still pained him so severely that he had become an aspirin addict" (42-43). Hickcock repeatedly swears, "I'm a normal" and, when Perry, reflecting on the murders, suggests that there just might be "something wrong" with them after all, Hickock denies it with all the self-righteousness of a teetotaling old aunt. Yet Hickock runs over dogs on the highway and "promises" Smith, when planning the robbery, that there will be "lots of hair on them-those walls" (50). Hickock is the one with the "sexual interest in female children" who wants to stop, in the middle of the burglary, to rape Nancy Clutter (229). For his part, Smith rather typically, if pathetically, fantasizes about "theatrical" fame, envisioning himself as Perry O'Parsons, "The One-Man Symphony," with a white top hat and a white tuxedo, with songs and instruments and tap dance steps attuned to every nuance of popular taste (62, 357). Yet he also continues to dream of the yellow parrot, his projection of isolated vengeance—and his two fantasies eventually flow together in front of an audience of "phantoms, the ghosts of the legally annihilated, the hanged, the gassed, the electrocuted" (357).

Most importantly, Capote includes the detailed psychological profiles that the defense attorney's expert witnesses would have provided, if the law had not prevented them from doing so. Most tellingly, so far as the community is concerned, Capote even includes passages from an article, "Murder Without Apparent Motive—A Study in Personality Disorganization," written by Joseph Satten in collaboration with three of his colleagues. After criticizing the ordinary legal distinctions between the "sane" and the "insane," this article describes a "specific syndrome" that would apply, Satten thinks, to Smith and Hickock. Not surprisingly, by this point in the novel, this "syndrome" seems to apply almost equally to the local community. The psychologists write of a "lapse in ego control which makes possible the open expression of primitive violence" (335), and an "unconscious traumatic configuration" that "unwittingly sets into motion ... homicidal potential" (338). The murder of the ultra-respectable Clutters, followed by the capture of two young men who fit so well into the role of sacrificial victim, was just such a "configuration"—just such a psychological accident.

As Capote should have known, judging by his attention to such accidents throughout the book, the implications of this "testimony" are much more disturbing than either alien invaders or distrustful neighbors. Capote is not particularly determined to demonstrate that, in this particular case, justice has been denied in the courtroom. He never tries to prove that the unfortunate backgrounds of Smith and Hickock can really be used to explain why they became murderers, or even to give guidance on what sort of punishment would be appropriate for them. Instead, by including such a wide range of excluded, more or less psychiatric "testimony," he portrays the trial as little more than an official sanction to ensure that the execution will take place. In doing so, Capote demonstrates that violence is not just a foreign threat, something from "outside normal life." Sacrificial violence is the culmination of the sense of normalcy that holds the town together.

But in the end, no one, not even Capote, really wants to face this reality. At the execution of Smith and Hickock, Agent Dewey—who has become, in the course of the novel, increasingly difficult to separate from Capote's conscience—is once again mysteriously disappointed. He "had anticipated a setting of suitable dignity" (378). More importantly, he "had imagined that with the deaths of Smith and Hickock, he would experience a sense of climax, release, of a design justly completed" (382). By this point in the novel, it is no longer surprising that this imagined design is shattered by real events.

It is surprising, however, that Capote himself, after all his efforts to confront the psychological barriers between the world of the murderers and the world of victims, is compelled to falsify the ending of his "nonfiction novel" by attaching a completely fictional final scene. At the end, Dewey and Susan Kidwell, the best friend of the Clutter's murdered daughter, meet on a sunny May afternoon at the cemetery where the Clutter family is buried. Dewey recalls this meeting as he stands in the prison warehouse, having been "invited" as one of the "twenty-odd witnesses" to "the ceremony" of Smith and Hickock's hanging (378). When Dewey opens his eyes to see Smith's "childish feet, tilted, dangling"—at the moment, that is, when he realizes just how wrought with fiction his hope for "a design justly completed" really is— his thoughts jump back to a pristine moment in the past, the imagined, "casual encounter" in Garden City's "formal cemetery" (382). There, in that "good refuge from a hot day," where "fields blaze with the gold-green fire of half-grown wheat," Dewey thinks proudly of his new home and his two sons, now "deep-voiced" and "as tall as their father" (382). Susan Kidwell, only a child at the trial, is now "a willowy girl with white-gloved hands, smooth cap of dark-honeyed hair, and long, elegant legs" (383). Sexual maturity, it seems, makes up for a lot. "Normalcy" is made to reassert itself, as though it were a force of nature. It is in this setting that the book closes. Transported from the prison warehouse by an act of "novelistic" magic, Dewey strolls through that warm field, "starting home ... toward the trees, and under them, leaving behind him the big sky, the whisper of wind voices in the wind-bent wheat" (384). Time, at least this suddenly fictional time, has finally brought all things to fullness, and has brought Dewey, like Capote, to some comforting sense of closure. All is pretty much well. The murders—and, more importantly, all the subsequent "whispers" of fear, suspicion, and vengeance—have been displaced into a distant past. Smith's dangling feet have disappeared.

So, in one act of relatively "pure fiction," Capote provides the kind of satisfaction that, he would always argue, an execution should not provide in reality. Even Capote, the eternal "outsider" who spent nearly six years interviewing and corresponding with Smith and Hickock, is finally controlled by the irresistible dynamics of community bonding. He, too, needs to impose the apparent meaning of a completed "design," needs to construct a sort of myth, to normalize and dissipate his awareness of the events surrounding the execution, perhaps even to ease his conscience for not having tried to stop it. Like the critics who praised him so early in his career, and like the citizens of Holcomb who contributed so much to his greatest work, Capote does not really want to consider the disturbing truth that *this* center of the American psyche, this vision of justice as a vengeful God who must be propitiated so that the "natural" and social order can be restored, is only reached by luck—or, to put it in his own terms, by "a psychological accident." And he does not want to admit that, even then, any consideration of this center is always resisted, if not entirely avoided, by our desire to distance ourselves from the need for violence that holds together our communities.

BIBLIOGRAPHY

Capote, Truman. *In Cold Blood*. New York: Signet, 1965.
Clarke, Gerald. *Capote: A Biography*. New York: Simon and Schuster, 1988.
Cleaver, Eldridge. *Soul On Ice*. New York: Delta, 1968.

Creeger, George R. *Animals in Exile: Imagery and Theme in Capote's In Cold Blood*. Center for Advanced Studies, Wesleyan University, 1967.

Franklin, H. Bruce. *The Victim as Criminal and Artist: Literature from the American Prison*. New York: Oxford University Press, 1978.

Girard, René. *Violence and the Sacred*. Trans. Patrick Gregory. Baltimore: The Johns Hopkins University Press, 1977.

Mailer, Norman. "Introduction" to Jack Henry Abbott's *In The Belly of The Beast*. New York: Random House, 1981.

———. *The Executioner's Song*. New York: Warner, 1979.

Malcolm X and Alex Haley. *The Autobiography of Malcolm X*. New York: Ballantine, 1964.

Palmer, C. B. "A Farmer Looks at Farming." *Truman Capote's In Cold Blood: A Critical Handbook*. Ed. by Irving Malin. Belmont, California: Wadsworth, 1968. 2-6.

Making Sense of Contemporary Reality:
The Construction of Meaning in the Nonfiction Novel

Rummaging through Watts in the aftermath of the ghetto riots of 1965 Thomas Pynchon finds himself in the midst of an unlikely occurrence: a local art festival being held at Markham Junior High School. One of the specimen on display there in particular attracts his attention:

> In one corner was this old, busted, hollow TV set with a rabbit-ears antenna on top; inside, where its picture tube should have been, gazing out with scorched wiring threaded like electronic ivy among its crevices and sockets, was a human skull. The name of the piece was "The Late, Late, Late Show."[1]

This odd concoction of readymade and pop art, of objet trouvés and black humor with distinct apocalyptic overtones in many ways embodies the aesthetic preferences of the 1960s. Drawing on Modernist assumptions, art and reality are no longer thought of as separate domains. While some consider the project of art to be an altogether dubious endeavor, others favor the plain materiality of common experience over flights of the imagination. In literature, this gave rise to a body of works alternately labeled "New Journalism, nonfiction literature, literary nonfiction, factual fiction, faction" or "journalit."[2]

From *Historiographic Metafiction in Modern American and Canadian Literature.* © 1994 by Ferdinand Schöningh, Paderborn.

Late in 1969, Alfred Kazin reflects on the literature of the closing decade and concludes: "Writing about the 1960's, a period more notable for its social turmoil than for its belief in high art, I suggest that too much pressure on the individual writer by 'society' may be enough to document (not to 'explain') a notable absence of masterpieces."[3] This is not the place to engage in rankings or dismissals of alleged masterpieces. On the other hand, Kazin's assumption that art and societal pressures are mutually exclusive should not be taken for granted. One possible way for the artist to cope with societal pressures could be to confront them head-on and this is what some writers such as Norman Mailer, Truman Capote, Tom Wolfe, John Hersey, Joan Didion among others chose to do. In a way, they became field workers out to explore the upheavals, transformations, oddities and hitherto unrecognized areas of contemporary American life.

During the 1960s, a deluge of factual reports, oral histories, documents, investigative journalism, anthropological field work and experiential hyper-realism was presented to an American reading public which, according to Dwight Macdonald, was mostly "obsessed with technique, hagridden by Facts, in love with information."[4] Right next to the apparently rampant empiricism of the decade, some writers turned their attention to the immediacies of contemporary reality and by declaring these to be worthwhile subjects of art, they either sought to rejuvenate the tradition of social realism and/or to offer an alternative to the, from their point-of-view, anemic elitism and aloofness of experimental writing.[5] There are, of course, historical antecedents to this trend. The most conspicuous parallel can be drawn to the writing of the 1930s, another decade during which many writers felt compelled to abstain from the invention of fictional worlds and to turn to documentary modes of expression instead.[6]

The 1960s in America, and this is as commonplace as it is true, showed little, if any respect for established traditions, values and conventions. In the field of literature, the discursive boundaries between fiction, journalism and social science came increasingly under siege. Writers turned into reporters and/or social scientists, journalists claimed artistic merit for their work and social scientists trespassed the narrow confines of their disciplines. The anthropologist Oscar Lewis could thus claim that the oral histories collected in his book *The Children of Sánchez* represent a happy concurrence of scientific case study and art. Lewis prophetically proclaimed that "the tape recorder, used in taking down the life stories in this book, has made possible the beginning of a new kind of literature of social realism."[7] In a similar prophetic mood, Truman Capote advertised journalism as "the most avant-garde form of writing existent today" and as "the last great unexplored literary frontier."[8] It was finally Tom Wolfe's predictable role as the New Journalism's elder statesman to claim that in the course of the 1960s journalists had taken hold of the top rungs of literary prominence and, in the process, had wiped out "the novel as literature's main event."[9] Self-serving prophesies and hegemonic claims aside, it is clear that the various modes applied to record reality reflected the almost delirious immediacy of the period. Documentary writing thrived on its fascination with firsthand experience, its topicality and its frequently iconoclastic perspectives on events.

One form that the documentary writing of the 1960s and 1970s took was to revive the methods and the rhetoric of Muckraking journalism from the beginning of the century.[10] The contemporary Muckrakers resuscitated the turn-of-the-century progressivist agenda of healing society by exposing its wounds and suggesting appropriate remedies. Michael Harrington's *The Other America* (1962), John Hersey's *The Algiers Motel Incident* (1968) and Gail Sheehy's *Hustling* (1974) continue the kind of social exposé familiar since Jacob Riis' *How the Other Half Lives* (1890), Ida Tarbell's *History of the Standard Oil Company* (1904) or Erskine Caldwell's and Margaret Bourke-White's *You Have Seen Their Faces* (1937). Like their predecessors, these authors appeal to sentiments of redemption through revelation and renewal which had regained currency since the proclamation of John F. Kennedy's "New Frontier." Moral outrage, anger and shame on the part of the educated and well-to-do are strategically invoked as the key prerequisites for social reform.

John Hersey's *The Algiers Motel Incident* takes one episode from the Detroit ghetto riots of 1967 to pursue the subject of racial conflict. His in-depth reconstruction of the killing of three Black ghetto youths by Detroit policemen is presented alternately as meticulous report, as a parable on the vicissitudes of racial prejudice and as a moral and political lesson in the education of the author. The book is primarily based on the author's personal research into the events depicted. Hersey, who was once the seasoned war correspondent from nearly all battle grounds of World War II, appears in *The Algiers Motel Incident* as the somewhat baffled, insecure and highly self-conscious narrator of events. The sheer mass of evidence to be filtered, contradictory versions of the events by participants and the cultural barriers between Blacks and Whites contribute to Hersey's unease. One strategy he adopts is to shift the burden of the narrative to his informants. In the light of the social urgency of the subject and Hersey's declared ambition to reach "total conviction" he insists that "the story would have to be told as much as possible in the words of the participants."[11] *The Algiers Motel Incident* is for the most part told in the recorded speech of those who lived through the experience. Hersey arranges selected passages of informant narrative which serve to reconstruct the chronology of events and to provide commentary on the larger subject of race conflict. Other kinds of documents such as court testimony, police reports, newspaper articles or specialists' expertise complete the account. In addition, Hersey inserts a highly scrupulous and self-conscious narrative voice which comments on the credibility of informants, reflects on its own narrative method and offers tentative conclusions. While the documentary evidence remains foregrounded throughout the book, the shaping presence of the author is just as noticeable. Apparently, Hersey proceeds on the assumption that documents and participants are better suited to speak authoritatively about real events than outside observers, but he also carefully delineates the process of composition which gave rise to the text. The constant threat of fragmentation posed by the necessity to arrange diverse voices and other kinds of empirical evidence is held in check by chronological structure and the author's assumed role as a self-reflective center of perception.

Although Hersey goes into painstaking detail about his principles of research and composition, he leaves little doubt about the limitations of his account when he cautions the reader:

> Let not any of this suggest to you that I have been trying to persuade you, in the fraudulent tradition of American journalism, that I have been, or shall be, "objective." There is no such thing as objective reportage. Human life is far too trembling-swift to be reported in whole; the moment the recorder chooses nine facts out of ten he colors the information with his views. (*AMI*, 27)

This mood of epistemological uncertainty may come as a surprise to readers of Hersey's earlier journalism. Despite the wide-ranging empirical effort that went into the making of *The Algiers Motel Incident*, Hersey's claims for the veracity of his account are decidedly modest. The impressive quantity of gathered evidence does not by itself yield so-called self-evident truths. Rather than presenting his version of the killings of the three ghetto youths as final or authoritative, Hersey proceeds on the conviction "that every scrap of understanding, every door-crack glimmer of illumination, every thread that may lead not just to survival of the races but to health—all should be shared as soon as possible" (*AMI*, 28). Quite consistently with the tradition of Muckraking journalism, Hersey's exposure of racial violence hopes to initiate a process of moral regeneration on the part of the reader. His book aims at "the minds of men" (*AMI*, 29) who are invited to examine the evidence of the Algiers case, to challenge their own biases and ignorance and to contribute to a more desirable state of public affairs.

Norman Mailer, on the other hand, has never written to move anybody's heart or mind, at least not in any obvious way. His prime interest has been to explore the subcurrents of a media-mediated culture and the complexities of individual consciousness as they relate to collective experience. As a specimen for interrogation he has preferred to concentrate on his own consciousness, which he dissects in his writing in its various complementary or antagonistic facets. Mailer's often buffoonish ways of self-dramatization correspond to his self-image as a man who habitually "bobbed in waves of controversy like a cork with a comic dent."[12] *The Armies of the Night* (1968) is Mailer's participant observer report of the Vietnam War protests staged in Washington, D.C., in October of 1967. Mailer here assumes the role of the radical, not altogether happy, in a pinstripe suit who finds himself painfully torn between engagement and reflection. As he explains himself: "I was trying to bring a consciousness to America about the war in Vietnam through personifying a reasonably complicated middle-aged man caught up in the peace movement and not altogether willingly."[13] The result is a text which combines observation and participation, report and reflection, events and their symbolic representations. Rhetorically, Mailer shifts between apodictic statements, argumentative reasoning, pondering self-introspection and open speculation.

The title *The Armies of the Night* is taken from Matthew Arnold's "Dover Beach" (1851). In Arnold's poem an exalted moment of nature experience leads to an apocalyptic vision of a decaying world. Similarly, Mailer's perception of the anti-war protests is decidedly gloomy. Not only does he adopt Arnold's elegiac tone at times, but he also seems to share Arnold's visions of decay and of societal interaction as an erratic clash of disoriented forces. Mailer keeps at a distance the army of liberals, leftists, pacifists, students and hippies who have gathered in the capital to express their protest against the war. His attitude is ambivalent, sometimes disapproving, yet never static. In a coupling of observation and self-introspection, Mailer shifts between brusque distance and understanding sympathy.

Mailer has a keen sense of the theatricality of the events around him and of "the thicket of unreality which stands between us and the facts of life."[14] His depiction of the protest march stresses the performatory dimension of social action:

> After fifteen minutes of pushing, eddying, compressing and decompressing from ranks, the march at last started up in a circus-full of performers, an ABC or CBS open convertible with a built-on camera platform was riding in privileged position five yards in front of them with TV executives, cameramen, and technicians hanging on, leaning out, off on their own crisis run as they crawled along in front.[15]

In the presence of the media, every statement is subject to abbreviation and distortion and every action will be reduced to an image or two. Following the laws of the "aesthetic economy of symbolic gestures" (*AN*, 182) Mailer carefully stages his own arrest. After having considered various alternatives, he finally decides to cross a rope and face the nearest policeman. His arrest marks the transition from radical talk to radical action, from legal protest to real and symbolic illegality. Mailer's self-perception at the time of his arrest captures the ambiguity of self-conscious performance and action:

> It was as if the air had changed, or light had altered; he felt immediately much more alive—yes, bathed in air—and yet disembodied from himself, as if indeed he were watching himself in a film where this action was taking place. He could feel the eyes of the people behind the rope watching him, could feel the intensity of their existence as spectators. (*AN*, 147)

Critics have often chided Mailer for his alleged egocentrism or narcissistic foregrounding of the self. In *The Armies of the Night* Mailer successfully integrates self-reflection with nuanced reportage. His calculated dramatization of so many facets of the self, often brought forth in a self-ironical mood, serves well to shed light on the tensions between inner drama and outside events, between imagination and reality.[16] Mailer's ruminations on his own "endless blendings of virtue and corruption" (*AN*, 74f.) contribute to a generative discourse in which the associativity of subjective consciousness is engaged for the presentation of a complex vision.

When authors turn into field workers, the reality they set out to record becomes magnified by their very presence. Reconstructions of spectacular criminal cases invariably bear the signature of their architects, regardless of whether they are offered as fictionalized accounts such as Edgar Allan Poe's "The Mystery of Marie Roget" (1842) and Theodore Dreiser's *An American Tragedy* (1925) or as unabashed "documentary" such as Meyer Levin's *Compulsion* (1956), Truman Capote's *In Cold Blood* (1966) and Norman

Mailer's *The Executioner's Song* (1979). In recent times, Capote and Mailer have both dealt with real-life affairs of violence and crime. Their examples show that the documentation of crimes does not only pose compositional problems, but that the reporter himself may very well become entangled in the reality he merely means to record. At the outset, certain similarities between the cases chosen by Capote and Mailer and their modes of presentation are apparent. Both authors deal with murders of extraordinary brutality. In both cases, the committed crimes shatter worlds of respectable conventionality. The commonality of the victims heightens the horror of their deaths. Erratically operating killers find their victims by accident or default rather than by choice or coherent scheme. Capote and Mailer both focus on the biographies or psychopathologies of the criminals. They unravel highly nuanced personality profiles of the killers which cast the reader into a limbo of repulsion and compassion, of condemnation and sympathy. Moreover, both accounts show a certain fixation on the details of police investigation, on the drama of chase and arrest, on courtroom proceedings and on the ordeals of eternal stays of execution. In these respects, they follow the familiar formulas according to which violent crimes are typically presented in film, TV series and popular crime novels.[17]

In the case of the nonfiction novel, the construction of meaning does not begin with the composition of the text, but prior to writing with the gathering of evidence. The selection of informants implies already a particular angle on the events to be reconstructed. The skill and sensitivity of the author as interviewer, his conduct in participant observation or the plain accessibility of sources will inevitably be reflected in the evidence. Also, the chosen informants will most likely be somewhat affected by the sudden limelight of public attention and they will act and speak accordingly.

Truman Capote's *In Cold Blood*, subtitled "A True Account of a Multiple Murder and Its Consequences," recounts the 1959 murder of the Clutter family in rural Kansas and its aftermath. During the 1950s a number of psychopathological killers such as Lena Nienstaedt, Kenneth Chapin and Charles Starkweather had gained notoriety and unhappy fame. Quickly baptized by the media as "thrill killers," these criminals chose their victims randomly, killed without recognizable scheme or interest and seemed to derive considerable pleasure from acts of violence and destruction. This particular pattern of crime, although not quite applicable to the Clutter case, must have been on Capote's mind when he first heard of the murders in Kansas through a brief article in the *New York Times*. Almost immediately Capote travelled to Kansas to do on-site research and conduct interviews with participants. Eventually, his activities, as well as the ensuing book, would focus on the actions and personalities of the criminals, as is most commonly done in all genres of crime depiction.

The credibility of Capote's tale rests considerably on the author's familiarity, if not intimacy with the two killers, Perry Smith and Richard Hickock, whom he first met immediately after their arrest and with whom he met and corresponded until their execution almost five years later. Capote indefatigably stressed his friendly relations with the two: "I did win their confidence and we became very close."[18] And, not without arrogance: "I knew them better than they knew themselves."[19] Predictably, Capote's conflicting roles as friend and detached chronicler led to what his biographer Gerald Clarke calls "an insoluble moral dilemma."[20] It is obvious that Capote could not publish his account of the Clutter murder until the case had come to some kind of conclusion. While a series of appeals and stays of execution dragged on, Capote's anxieties intensified. In September of 1963 he wrote to a friend: "I am in a really appalling state of tension and anxiety. Perry and Dick have an appeal for a new trial pending in Federal Court: if they should get it [a new trial] I will have a complete breakdown of some sort."[21] During the almost five years that Hickock and Smith lingered on death row, not once did Capote make an effort to actively support their repeated attempts to have the death sentences revoked. Some critics have speculated that Capote may have been more committed to the success of his book than to the fate of his convict friends.[22] When in the fall of 1964 Capote, with help from a staff member of *The New Yorker*'s legendary fact-checking department, was busy with final inspections on the factuality of his text, Hickock and Smith were engaged in last-ditch efforts to avert execution. It is of course vain to speculate on what might have happened if Capote had chosen a course of action more conducive to the interests of his friends. Moreover, a competent discussion of the issues involved here would require some technical expertise in Kansas and federal law, in criminological questions of mental health, etc. What should be obvious, however, is the fact that the act of recording reality can have considerable impact on that very reality. Observer and observed are inextricably wound up in the reality they both share and shape. Without Capote, Hickock and Smith would have remained more or less anonymous killers among many others. Capote's reluctance to act on behalf of the murderers and his friendly relations with them reverberate in real life and in the book. Also, the two convicts were more than just plain informants. At least Hickock's willingness to collaborate on the book was strategic, as Capote learned from his response to an early draft:

Dick's [Hickock] reaction to the book was to start switching and changing his story, saying what I had written wasn't exactly true. He wasn't trying to flatter himself; he tried to change it to serve his purposes legally, to support the various appeals he was sending through the courts. He wanted the book to read as if it was a legal brief for presentation in his behalf before the Supreme Court.[23]

In a way, Capote's failure as a friend assured his success as a writer. His detached style, the impersonal objectivity which he brought to his subject impressed readers and critics alike. Jimmy Breslin was one among many to stress this particular quality of *In Cold Blood*: "The important thing is it could affect the type of words on pages you could be reading for a while. This Capote steps in with flat, objective, terrible realism. And suddenly there is nothing else you want to read."[24] While Capote's stark prose is certainly well-suited to his documentary design, it should not be overlooked that his version of the Clutter case is at times derivative of fictional models and in conflict with available evidence. In the book, the murder of the Clutter family is not presented as a carefully planned and carried out crime, as the title would suggest. It is rather the tragic peak in the hapless lives of two misfits whose biographies Capote saw as being under the spell of "doom against which virtue was no defense."[25] Especially Perry Smith appears as the victim of a long series of frustrations and humiliations which had eventually muted his talents and promise. Capote characterizes Smith as a thoughtful, sensitive person with an artistic bent. Right before his execution, Smith is said to have apologized for his crimes. Capote quotes him with the following last words: "It would be meaningless to apologize for what I did. Even inappropriate. But I do. I apologize" (*ICB*, 340). Two other journalists who were present at the execution with Capote insist that Smith did not express regret.[26] Of course, it would be rash to favor anybody's testimony here. It is obvious, however, that the apology which Capote attributes to Smith ties in neatly with the portrayal of Smith as an ambiguous villain who is capable of evoking considerable sympathy and compassion.

Capote's depiction of the site of the crime in West Kansas brims with mythopoetic projection:

The village of Holcomb stands on the high wheat plains of western Kansas, a lonesome area that other Kansans call "out there." Some seventy miles east of the Colorado border, the countryside with its hard blue skies and desert-clear air, has an

atmosphere that is rather more Far West than Middle West.[...]
The land is flat, and the views are awesomely extensive; horses,
herds of cattle, a white cluster of grain elevators rising as
gracefully as Greek temples are visible long before a traveler
reaches them. (*ICB*, 3)

Obviously not content with the mere topography of the place, Capote
foregrounds atmospheric attributes such as remoteness, vastness and a
somewhat premonitory loneliness. In its atmospheric density and evocations
of ominous fatality much of Capote's narrative is reminiscent of "Southern
Gothic." The end of *In Cold Blood* is strikingly similar to that of Capote's
earlier novelette *The Grass Harp* (1951). Both texts conclude with an elegiac
cemetery scene where youth, age and the inevitability of death are brought
together. *In Cold Blood* ends with a chance encounter at the grave of the
victims between police officer Alvin Dewey and Susan Kidwell, Nancy
Clutter's best friend. Whether fabricated or real, the scene effectively closes
the cycle of destruction, mourning and new beginning.

Norman Mailer enjoys with *The Executioner's Song* (1979) all the
advantages and disadvantages of hindsight. His involvement in the subject
did not begin until after the execution of the murderer. The case of Gary
Gilmore had been headline news around the world in late 1976 and early
1977 when the convicted murderer had insisted on a speedy execution.
During his work on the book, Mailer became a "partner in crime" in a
peculiar way. When the convict Jack Henry Abbott learned that Mailer was
working on the Gilmore case, he wrote to Mailer and offered inside
knowledge into prison life. Mailer and Abbott corresponded for some time.
Eventually Mailer became active on behalf of Abbott for a release on parole.
Also, Mailer was impressed by Abbott's writing and helped him to get
published. Abbott's first book appeared in 1981 and turned an anonymous
convict into a celebrity.[27] Shortly after his early release from jail in the same
year, Abbott stabbed a waiter in a New York restaurant and Mailer became
the target of a vehement public campaign charging him with complicity in
varying degrees. Thus, another chronicler of reality became deeply
enmeshed in the world he had merely meant to record.[28]

The Executioner's Song is essentially two tales divided into two books,
"Western Voices" and "Eastern Voices." While the first book reconstructs
the life, crimes and punishments of Gary Gilmore, the second book is a
highly instructive lesson on the criminal case as a media event. Three days
before the execution Gilmore confides to his brother: "I didn't mean for it to
become such a big thing. I thought there would be a few articles."[29] The

convict on death row experiences mixed feelings. Satisfied on the one hand that the extent of public attention will assure him a place in "history," he has to realize on the other that the remainder of his life has been taken over by interests which he neither shares nor controls. As Gilmore was to learn, once the media is on to a lucrative case, facts and gossip become negotiable commodities and the press becomes an active agent in the world it is out to report. Participants of a crime—criminals, victims, witnesses alike—become owners of highly valued information. They are courted and flattered for their presumably privileged insights. Sometimes they find themselves transmogrified into showpieces and subjected to voyeuristic sensationalism.

The principal figure in book two of *The Executioner's Song*, "Eastern Voices," is Lawrence Schiller, a former photographer for *Life* magazine turned into a shady mercenary specializing in the commercialization of spectacular crimes. Schiller has managed to outdo his competitors and holds the exclusive rights on Gilmore's story, including those for film, TV and book publication. During Gilmore's ordeal, Schiller has set up an office in a motel near the prison where he employs lawyers, researchers and secretaries and from which he keeps in contact with the convict. Eventually Schiller was to obtain the collaboration of Norman Mailer for the planned book.

In most cases, nonfiction texts do not reveal the circumstances of their making. *The Executioner's Song* is a notable exception. Mailer makes extensive use of the evidence, trivia and drama provided by Schiller, but he also sheds light on the involvement of Schiller and the likes of him. His book is a compelling account of the potentially fatal entanglement of documentary interest, the proselytizing and exhibitory impact of the media and the event itself. Borrowing from Beckett's play "Krapp's Last Tape" (1959), one of Mailer's chapters is entitled "Gilmore's Last Tape." Mailer parodies the evidence on which his own text is largely based. A few hours before Gilmore's execution, Schiller is on the phone with the convict to secure last-minute insights into the mind of the criminal for posterity. The scene in Schiller's motel office is distinctly surreal:

> Next to Schiller, lying on the floor under the table, was Barry Farrell listening to the conversation through an earpiece attached by a short wire to the tape recorder. Schiller wanted to see Barry's face and get his reactions, but all he could manage from the angle at which he sat was the occasional sight of Barry's hand writing on a 3 x 5 card. (*ES*, 905)

In a certain sense, the criminal has become the victim of the reporter. Gilmore's story is extracted to the hilt. Moreover, his case becomes a parable on the compilation and construction of momentous tales. The reporter turns into a participating agent and assumes in this particular case a highly dubious role. As Diane Johnson suggests: "Indeed if it weren't for Gilmore's evident death wish one might feel that Schiller and his lawyers were responsible for his death in the way they played to his infantile us-against-them reactions to authority."[30]

Mailer's approach to the writing of the Gilmore case differs substantially from his documentary practice in such earlier books as *The Armies of the Night, Miami and the Siege of Chicago* or *Of A Fire on the Moon. The Executioner's Song* proceeds without the foregrounding of an authorial voice and without Mailer's customary predilection for self-dramatization. The prose appears depoeticized, plain and matter-of-fact. Against the horror of the events and the hysteria of public debate Mailer reaches for a flat and unadorned narrative style, such as in the depiction of the scene immediately after Gilmore's first murder:

> He [Gilmore] stood up. There was a lot of blood. It spread across the floor at a surprising rate. Some of it got onto the bottom of his pants.
>
> He walked out of the rest room with the bills in his pocket, and the coin changer in his hand, walked by the big Coke machine and the phone on the wall, walked out of this real clean gas station. (*ES*, 227)

A typical page in *The Executioner's Song* consists of several short and clearly marked off paragraphs. Mailer assembles narrative passages with interview transcripts, letters, police records, court testimony, news articles, etc. Shifts in time, place and point-of-view are frequent. One is, at times, led to suspect that Mailer merely passed on piles of filing cards with field notes for transcription. Mailer compiles evidence with a vengeance. No piece of data is too trivial, too private, too marginal not to qualify for inclusion in the text which amounts to more than 1,000 pages. The effect is a cacophony of voices never to be arranged into a coherent tale. Gary Gilmore's story does not even lend itself to a plot structure of tragedy. The structure of the book duplicates the impenetrable thicket of evidence surrounding the case and the incongruities of testimony. Coherence and plausibility are left strewn along the way. Mailer's technique of cutting and assembling evidence from multiple sources leads to a convergence of discourses which incessantly interfere with each other or give rise to other discourses. The result is a discursive world clearly out-of-bounds—a message which was not lost on Gilmore himself. In letters to his girlfriend he observed: "Honey, I'm becoming very famous. I don't like it—not like this, it's not right" (*ES*, 549). And in another letter: "It's all become like a circus" (*ES*, 545).

NOTES

1. Thomas Pynchon, "A Journey into the Mind of Watts," *The New Journalism*, ed. Nicolaus Mills (New York, 1974), 52.

2. Among the monographs on the subject are Chris Anderson, *Style As Argument* (Carbondale, 1987); John Hellmann, *Fables of Fact* (Urbana, 1981); John Hollowell, *Fact & Fiction* (Chapel Hill, 1977); Barbara Lounsberry, *The Art of Fact* (New York, 1990); Ronald Weber, *The Literature of Fact* (Athens, OH, 1980); Mas'ud Zavarzadeh, *The Mythopoeic Reality* (Urbana, 1976).

3. Alfred Kazin, "The Literary Sixties, When the World Was Too Much With Us," *The New York Times Book Review* (December 21, 1969), B7, 1.

4. Dwight Macdonald, *Against the American Grain* (New York, 1983), 393.

5. See also Jost Hermand, "Wirklichkeit als Kunst: Pop, Dokumentation und Reportage," *Basis*, 2 (1971), 33-52.

6. The best source on 1930s documentary is William Stott, *Documentary Expression and Thirties America* (Chicago, 1973).

7. Oscar Lewis, *The Children of Sánchez* (New York, 1963), xii.

8. *Truman Capote: Conversations*, ed. M. Thomas Inge (Jackson, 1987), 121f.

9. Tom Wolfe, "The New Journalism," *The New Journalism*, ed. Tom Wolfe and E.W. Johnson (New York, 1973), 9 and 23.

10. For an account of contemporary Muckraking see Leonard Downie, *The New Muckrakers* (Washington, 1976).

11. John Hersey, *The Algiers Motel Incident* (New York, 1968), 27; hereafter *AMI*.

12. Norman Mailer, *The Prisoner of Sex* (Boston, 1971), 30.

13. Laura Adams, "Existential Aesthetics: An Interview with Norman Mailer," *Partisan Review*, 42 (1975), 208.

14. Daniel J. Boorstin, *The Image—A Guide to Pseudo-Events in America* (New York, 1961), 3.

15. Norman Mailer, *The Armies of the Night* (New York, 1968), 132; hereafter *AN*.

16. See also Warner Berthoff, "Witness and Testament: Two Contemporary Classics," *New Literary History*, 2 (1970/71), 324.

17. See also Hans Joachim Schneider, *Das Geschäft mit dem Verbrechen: Massenmedien und Kriminalität* (München, 1980), 10.

18. Inge, *Capote*, 123.

19. Ibid., 214.

20. Gerald Clarke, *Capote: A Biography* (New York, 1988), 352.

21. Clarke, *Capote*, 349.

22. See for example Kenneth Tynan, "The Kansas Farm Murders," *London Observer* (March 13, 1966), 21, and Capote's reply "The Guts of a Butterfly," *London Observer* (March 27, 1966), n.p. Also Elisabeth Plessen, "*In Cold Blood*: Synopsis einer Kontroverse anläßlich eines Non-Fiction-Romans von Truman Capote," *Akzente*, 14 (1967), 511-520.

23. Inge, *Capote*, 57.

24. Quoted after Clarke, *Capote*, 365.

25. Truman Capote, *In Cold Blood* (New York, 1965), 185; hereafter *ICB*.

26. See Philip K. Tompkins, "In Cold Fact," *Esquire*, 65 (June 1966), 170.

27. Jack Henry Abbott, *In the Belly of the Beast* (New York, 1981).

28. See also Stephen Greenblatt, "Capitalist Culture and the Circulatory System," *The Aims of Representation*, ed. Murray Krieger (New York, 1987), 269-271.

29. Norman Mailer, *The Executioner's Song* (New York, 1980), 834; hereafter *ES*.

30. Diane Johnson, "Death for Sale," *The New York Review of Books* (December 6, 1979), 4.

JOHN HOLLOWELL

Capote's In Cold Blood: *The Search for Meaningful Design*

However long it takes, it may be the rest of my life, I'm going to know what happened in that house: the why and the who.
                    —Alvin Dewey, Chief Detective

I have finished the book, but in a sense I *haven't* finished it: it keeps churning around in my head. It particularizes itself now and then, but not in the sense that it brings about a total conclusion.
                    —Capote, *New York Times Book Review*, 16 January 1966

In early studies of the new journalism and the nonfiction novel, critics have sought to identify the fictional techniques that make the nonfiction novel "read" like a novel. In *The New Journalism*, Tom Wolfe speaks of the realistic novel's "emotional involvement," or its "gripping" and "absorbing" quality (31). Perhaps the most often cited of these devices of realism, according to Wolfe, is "scene by scene reconstruction and resorting as little as possible to sheer historical narration" (31). The supposed effect on the reader is a reconstruction of events with full dialogue and psychological depth without the anonymous summary or narration of traditional journalism.

More recent readers of Capote's *In Cold Blood* have discussed the degree of closure and resolution such scenes achieve with respect to reading the

From *Arizona Quarterly* 53, no. 3 (Autumn 1997). © 1997 by the Arizona Board of Regents.

overall meaning of the Clutter murders. Brian Conniff, for example, examines the crucial role of what he calls psychological accidents in the recreation of the crimes and Capote's overall narrative plan (74–94), while Phyllis Frus adopts the opposing view that Capote's method allows for the murders to be explained and rationalized within a framework of middle-class ideology and psychological analysis (120–56). I want to explore the category of "meaningful design," apparently drawn from Detective Dewey's verbal world, since it strategically offers an explanatory framework for understanding murder. In fact, the careful construction of the confession, trial, and execution scenes refers to this standard, one that promises to resolve vexing questions for readers of *In Cold Blood*. Capote's strategy, however, is to raise the possibility of rational order without ever fully endorsing it, often revealing that random and accidental events shape the history of the crime. Capote's narrative method also emphasizes two language systems—the first based on punishment, the second on psychological analysis of personality—that demonstrate opposing ways of judging human behavior. This conflict undermines any straightforward rational design for comprehending murder or its punishment. To evaluate these issues of closure and meaning in *In Cold Blood*, I examine three critical scenes in detail—the confessions of the killers, the courtroom verdicts, and the executions—to provide the best opportunity to identify a total-ized, clear sense of an ending.

Until Part 3 of the book, "Answer," Capote's method emphasizes the mysterious, evasive nature of the crimes and their effects on the towns folk of Holcomb, Kansas. The three scenes I have selected are presented through the eyes of Alvin Dewey, the law-and-order hero of the book. Since Capote's narrative method does not allow the author to speak in his own, first-person voice, Dewey acts as the central intelligence guiding our integration of plot elements. The reader is likely to identify with Dewey's viewpoint as she identifies with Dewey's search for design, since it will presumably create an explanatory framework that will allow her to understand the bizarre murders. These three scenes provide a basis for reading the murders, for placing them within a coherent design for *In Cold Blood* as a whole. The narrative promises to create an understanding of the crimes and get to the bottom of the killers' motives—if not through the legal system, then perhaps through the process of psychological analysis. Dewey's role is critical since his motives and desires allow readers to identify with the eventual capture and punishment of the suspects.

The confession scene develops in "Answer" when Dick Hickock and Perry Smith are arrested in Las Vegas as their cross-country ride comes to an end; Capote signals the arrival of a dramatic climax in which we may find out "what really happened." It is useful to study the staging *words* and interviews in some depth, both for the portrait of Dewey's actions and for our understanding of the motivation and possible logic behind the crimes. First, recall that Capote's narrative strategy left the black Chevrolet frozen in moonlight in the Clutter driveway on the night of the murders, but the murders have never been described "in real time." Second, the confession scene promises to release pent-up curiosity about the crimes, which up to this point have been presented as motiveless and inexplicable. Our anticipation takes its cue from Dewey's solemn vow when first encountering the murder scene: "However long it takes, it may be the rest of my life, I'm going to know what happened in that house: the why and the who" (*In Cold Blood* 80).

Dewey's thoughts about the case suggest a rational framework for understanding murder—a meaningful design. The possibility of this design comes from the general human need for meaning and the specific need for closure, to put an ending to a series of plausible yet always puzzling explanations. Second, Capote's strategy raises the possibility of design and meaning by strengthening the reader's identification with Detective Dewey, who dominates every phase of the case. What I propose is to examine the confession, the trial, and the execution scenes against the standard of meaning Dewey envisions. Capote's treatment of this complex standard of resolution is linked to any interpretation of *In Cold Blood* and its overall aesthetic effects.

One test to apply to the confession and the trial scenes is the extent to which rational explanation—the why and the who—appears in the final revelation of the crimes in "Answer." On December 30, 1959, after more than six weeks of cluelessness and frustration, Dewey learns of Hickock and Smith's arrest in Las Vegas. While this should be an occasion for joy in the Dewey family, Alvin remains pessimistic that the case will finally be solved since the physical evidence is slim: "Yes, a big lot of good they [photographs of bloody footprints] are ... unless those boys still happen to be wearing those boots that made them" (213). Reflecting on the flimsy evidence as he dresses for a quick departure for Las Vegas with his three Kansas Bureau of Investigation partners, Dewey tells his wife the only interviewing strategy he can think of: "the name Clutter has to hit them like a hammer, a blow they never knew was coming" (213). Such a statement anticipates a fierce struggle between law enforcement and criminals who had hoped to leave no clues behind.

Capote allows the *why* of the crimes to play itself out slowly, since at first the two suspects are allowed to believe they have been arrested for minor violations of parole and hot check writing. In Capote's chosen order, Hickock is the first to be interrogated by agents Church and Nye. After pursuing the check-writing incidents in Kansas City, Church mentions the weekend of November 14–15, while Hickock rambles on with a prepared false alibi about traveling to Fort Scott to see Smith's sister and picking up two prostitutes. By allowing Hickock to exhibit "his one true gift" of recollection, the detectives let him go on to name all the roads, hotels, and highways from Kansas to Florida, and back through Texas to Nevada. Nye then zeroes in on him: "I guess you realize we wouldn't have come all the way to Nevada to chat with a couple of two-bit check chiselers" (222). Capote cites the detectives' contemporaneous notes of the moment when Nye mentions the name "Clutter": "Suspect underwent an intense visible reaction. He turned gray" (223). The two detectives then deliver a blow intended to shatter Hickock's alibi:

> "But you made two mistakes, Dick. One was, you left a witness. A living witness. Who'll testify in court. Who'll stand in the witness box and tell a jury how Richard Hickock and Perry Smith bound and gagged and slaughtered four helpless people." (223)

While he is visibly rattled, Hickock still denies any knowledge of the murders. Detectives Nye and Church decide to cut off the interview, allowing him to brood over his guilt and a possible death sentence. Capote's interest lies in the methods of trapping suspects and forcing a confession. His goal is to dramatize the pressure applied by the detectives and Dick's wavering motives for confessing or withholding information.

When first confronted with the idea of a witness, Hickock thinks of an *eyewitness*—someone who actually saw the crime—and he soon remembers his old cellmate, Floyd Wells, but dismisses any danger figuring that "the sonofabitch was probably expecting some fancy reward" (227). Detectives finally break down Dick's protestations of innocence, however, by showing him large "one to one" blowup photographs of the bloody footprints from the murder scene, and he quickly realizes that Smith is the one witness who could damage him the most: "It was *Perry* he ought to have silenced. On a mountain road in Mexico. Or while walking across the Mojave" (228). When Hickock contemplates the photographs of the crime scene and considers their use in court, he blurts out: "'Perry Smith killed the Clutters.... It was Perry. I couldn't stop him. He killed them all'" (230). The interrogation of Hickock reflects his desire to hold out in the face of his fear of Smith and the physical evidence. He attempts to exculpate himself by declaring that he did not actually kill any member of the family. Capote shows Hickock's thinking as he falls back on the claim that he did not actually pull the trigger and therefore should not be charged with first-degree murder.

Capote soon switches the interrogation to Smith, since his version of events promises to answer Dewey's questions about motive. Following a similar reconstructive method throughout, Capote develops Smith's testimony more completely than Hickock's, reporting in the present tense to intensify the immediacy. After more than three hours of questioning, Agent Duntz tells Smith that on November 14, "'You were killing the Clutter family'" (225), but Smith stubbornly sticks to the cover story about Fort Scott and the prostitutes. Finally, Dewey decides to cut the interview off, leaving Smith with the guilt-inducing knowledge that the next day would have been Nancy Clutter's birthday: "'She would have been seventeen'" (226).

In portraying Smith in this section, Capote uses the most controversial technique of the nonfiction novel. Instead of quoting directly or using typical journalistic attribution, he adopts a point of view coming from inside the suspect's mind. While it seems as if an omniscient author has access to his private thoughts, everything Smith "thinks" came from extensive interviews Capote conducted much later on Death Row. Here Smith worries about Hickock's ability to hold out against sharp interrogation.

> ... well, he damn near died, that's all. He must have lost ten pounds in two seconds. Thank God he hadn't let them see it. Or hoped he hadn't. And Dick? Presumably they'd pulled the same stunt on him. Dick was smart, a convincing performer, but his "guts" were unreliable, he panicked too easily. Even so, and however much they pressured him, Perry was sure that Dick would hold out. (227)

While Smith avoids confessing in Las Vegas, he finally breaks down and tells the "whole story" during his transport back to Kansas. Dewey inadvertently tells Smith that Hickock has spoken of "King," a black man whom Smith supposedly whipped to death in a false story he made up to impress Hickock. At first, Smith cannot believe Hickock has confessed to any involvement in the Clutter case: "'I thought it was a stunt. I didn't believe you. That Dick let fly. The tough boy!'" (232). But the revelation about the King story becomes a critical signal because if Hickock ever confessed, "'dropped his guts all over the goddamn floor—I knew he'd tell about the nigger'" (232).

This revelation launches Smith's narration into the events on the night of the murders. Dewey is attentive, having sworn to himself long ago to learn every detail of the murders, hoping for a coherent story to resolve his doubts and earlier confusion. Since the outset of the long investigation of the senseless murders, the reader follows Dewey's reactions with hope that the dramatic highlights of the book will occur in this scene. As Dewey performs the repellent act of lighting cigarettes for the handcuffed Smith, the two factors that dominate the story of the night of the murders are the bickering and macho posturing of the two men, and the obvious fact that Mr. Clutter kept no safe at his house.

Far from being a portrayal of two homicidal maniacs on a rampage, what is striking about Smith's narrative are odd moments of quiet, moments of hesitation when the whole scheme might have been ended without anyone dying. In the driveway, both men swig from a bottle of whiskey; Hickock says, "'I'll show you who's got guts,'" as the two muster courage for tying and gagging each member of the family, the women upstairs and Kenyon and Mr. Clutter in the basement (235). When it becomes apparent that there is no office safe, and Smith understands that the "big score" is a bust, he reports wanting just to leave the house: "'Why don't I walk off? Walk to the highway, hitch a ride. I sure Jesus did not want to go back in that house'" (240). But there is an odd magnet, according to Smith, almost as if he is watching someone other than himself: "'It was like I wasn't part of it. More as though I was reading a story. And I had to know what was going to happen. The end'" (240). Seeing himself in the role of spectator is a bizarre feature of Smith's narration, implying that he is watching some other person commit the crimes.

This curious dissociation of thoughts and emotions from actions permeates much of Smith's account of the night of November 14. Later, in the psychiatric analysis, it will be presented as a case of Smith's "magical thinking," his uncanny ability to separate and distance himself from events and action, as if he were watching a movie in which he was a character. Early on, Perry talks of shaking down Nancy Clutter's room and the shame of searching for her souvenir silver dollar: "'... it rolled across the floor. Rolled under a chair. I had to get down on my knees. And just then it was like I was outside myself. Watching myself in some nutty movie. It made me sick.... Dick, and all his talk about a rich man's safe, and here I am crawling on my belly to steal a child's silver dollar'" (240). Again, Capote's report of Smith's confession emphasizes the feeling of being "outside himself," as if he were watching some "movie." Capote dwells on the silver dollar incident because

Smith himself understands it as a symbol of the absurdity of the theft, a shameful reminder of pointless torture and murder.

Despite the high points of action in Smith's story—the killing of Mr. Clutter, the rapid shotgun blasts—the length of time in the house with strange moments of quiet lead us to a discomfiting series of *what ifs*. Readers are cued to wait for a design that will explain the motive for the murders. For example, Smith tells of ordering Hickock to leave Nancy's room for "'that's something I despise. Anybody that can't control themselves sexually'" (243). Yet when Dick leaves the room, Perry has a surreal yet quite "normal" conversation with a girl who fears for her life:

> "She was trying hard to act casual and friendly. I really liked her. She was really nice. A very pretty girl, and not spoiled or anything. She told me quite a lot about herself. About school, and how she was going to go to a university and study music and art. Horses. Said next to dancing what she liked best was to gallop a horse, so I mentioned my mother had been a champion rodeo rider." (242)

This is an odd conversation, for here is a nice girl that Perry's criminal life has never allowed him to meet and, ironically, he is able to have a friendly chat about horses in the moments just before killing her at point-blank range. Readers may have difficulty resolving such a moment with the rapid series of shotgun blasts, and the sudden flash of anger that remains uncanny.

After telling of several such moments of pause and quiet, Smith mentions the final strategy session between the two men just before the killing of Mr. Clutter, the first in the chain reaction of killing. With the lights out and the family taped and bound, Smith presents this huddle as a prelude to the actual murders:

> "Dick and I went off in a corner. To talk it over. Remember, now, there were hard feelings between us. Just then it made my stomach turn to think I had ever admired him.... I said, 'Well Dick. Any qualms?' He didn't answer me. I said, 'Leave them alive, and this won't be any small rap. Ten years the very least.'... I asked him for [the knife], and he gave it to me, and I said, 'All right, Dick. Here goes.' But I didn't mean it. I meant to call his bluff." (244)

Shortly after this point, Smith tells of Mr. Clutter struggling "half out of his ropes" and making a gurgling sound "like somebody drowning," while Smith dares Hickock to finish killing him. In Smith's version, he takes the knife from Hickock and then uses the shotgun to kill Mr. Clutter to end his suffering:

> "Dick wanted to get the hell out of there. But I wouldn't let him go. The man would have died anyway, I know that, but I couldn't leave him like he was. I told Dick to hold the flashlight, focus it. Then I aimed the gun. The room just exploded. Went blue. Just blazed up." (244)

As Smith finishes his story, Agent Dewey's ears "ring with it," and he knows that he has wanted these details all along since this case had begun to dominate his life. Every event of the confessions—all the terrors of the victims, every shotgun blast—has been presented. Yet has the story actually fulfilled the design Dewey so desires? Does the scene as reported reveal the *true answer* of "the why and the who" that Dewey sought? Recall that from the early scattering of disconnected clues, Dewey formulated two "concepts," one involving a single killer and another involving two or more men. These two scenarios demonstrate how even Dewey's crime-solving skills could not anticipate or comprehend what these particular killers were capable of. Because of the amount of taping and tying the family suffered, Dewey favored the "double-killer concept," but earlier he found it unbelievable that "'two individuals could reach the same degree of rage, the kind of psychopathic rage it took to commit such a crime'" (82—83). Even if someone had an insane rage against Herb Clutter, "'where did he find a partner, someone crazy enough to help him? It doesn't add up. It doesn't make sense'" (83). And yet, as he learns from Smith, this scenario is close to what happened.

Does Smith's confession add up to a story that makes sense now? Within this matrix of common sense and reason, Dewey does not feel satisfied with the answers. Even though all the details have been revealed, the murders remain outside an explanatory or rational viewpoint based on the human need for order that dominates Capote's approach. Capote shapes *In Cold Blood* to present the possibility of a rational view of murder and yet systematically denies or withdraws it. The narrative dwells on Dewey's sense of dissatisfaction, even after hearing every detail: "But the confessions, though they answered the questions of how and why, failed to satisfy [Dewey's] sense of meaningful design. The crime was a psychological accident, virtually an impersonal act; the victims might as well have been killed by lightning" (245).

Reviewing these moments of terror in the account Smith gives Dewey, we find a consistent failure to arrive at the "sense of meaningful design" Dewey is seeking. Each of the constituent elements leading to the moment of the crime is present: the failure to find a safe, the two men's anger toward each other, Smith's sense of shame, Hickock's embarrassment at not bringing off "the perfect score," the final thought that more prison time will surely await them if they leave witnesses and get caught. Each of these factors plays a role in the murders, yet no single motive in itself makes the killing necessary or inevitable. If any one of these elements had been missing, the murders might have been avoided; therefore, even by the end of the story things do not "add up" or "make sense."

As Brian Conniff has persuasively argued, the case would be too simple and indeed Capote's narrative would be too determined and obvious, like Dewey's two concepts, "if it were not for the intervention of certain 'accidents'" (77–94). Conniff goes on to show how Capote blurs the usual distinctions between good and evil. It is not excellent police work that solves the case but a "stroke of luck" when the convict Floyd Wells names Hickock. Dewey is lucky, too, that the killers are so foolish:

> ... by returning to their favorite hotels and continuing to pass bad checks, Smith and Hickock have just about guaranteed their own arrest outside a Las Vegas post office.... [Capote's method] provides the kind of juxtapositions that make the murderers' simple incompetence all the more glaring, in contrast to the elaborate suspicions and theories fostered by the "normal" community.... Perhaps it was only such events, combined with the trial and execution that would follow—in which "good" would stubbornly refuse to triumph over "evil," in which "sanity" would strangely refuse to explain and cure "insanity"—that could have forced [Capote] to question his initial design [for the book]. (Conniff 84–85)

Such commentary sheds light on what happens in the confession scene, because all the details make clear that the mystery does not follow the classic means of solving a murder—looking for motive and opportunity, nor does it adhere to the logic of Dewey's two prior concepts. In fact, rejecting the formula resolution of most crime stories, Capote endorses no clear-cut motive or reason for the murders. Crimes of premeditation can be understood, and even crimes of passion may be comprehensible in psychological terms. As in the classic literature of American crime—in Dreiser's *An American Tragedy*, for example, when Clyde Griffiths' pregnant fiancée drowns when the two of them are out rowing—events seem to *happen* without premeditation and beyond the conscious control of human agents.

Capote's narrator apparently offers us a false certainty when he says, "the confessions ... answered questions of how and why" (245), since a careful reader will seriously wonder if they do. A radical feature of Capote's book, one that has troubled many critics, is that the narrator never offers easy answers or a ready-made ethical framework for "understanding" the murders (Macdonald 44–48; Trilling 107–13). Hence, readers must confront the acts of terror and violence outside the framework of rational organization, while appreciating Garden City's long-awaited return to stability now that the perpetrators of the murders have been duly captured and jailed. As Capote sets up the equation, the dramatic work of the confessions helps establish the ground for another important scene, the trial in Garden City that once again promises to get to the bottom of the Clutter murders.

THE LAW VS. PSYCHOLOGY

If the confession scene does not fully satisfy the desire for "meaningful design," perhaps the trial of Hickock and Smith will provide the fuller explanation of the events that resist Dewey's sense of reason. Recent perspectives on language indicate that humans construct "reality" and "truth" from the vantage point of metaphorical and language systems that control our view of the world.[1] In the courtroom drama, for example, Capote manages to promote conflict by establishing two interpretations of the events—the first legal and restrictive, the second psychological—drawing arguments first from acts and then from a careful study of the killers' possible motivations. Both systems of language—the legal and the psychological—offer competing ways of reconstructing the past from different perspectives. The legal language focuses on action, responsibility, and laws of evidence—to determine whether the acts of murder were committed by these men. The psychological language provides psychiatric "testimony" to explore the unconscious motives for such "motiveless" crimes; the psychological testimony concerns personality structure and the formative events of childhood. Embedded in the psychiatric language is a definition of sanity that implicitly challenges the legal definition at the trial, by which Kansas law reduces matters to a simple yes-or-no answer.

At first glance, the outcome of the trial appears foregone: the physical evidence, the bloody photographs, the testimony of Floyd Wells, the careful reconstruction of the crime by Alvin Dewey, and the signed confessions all point to the guilt that will allow the community to restore its sense of order and quiet its fear by exacting guilty verdicts and the death penalty. The legal system, with its established rules of evidence, restricts what information can be presented to a jury. Crucial in this case is the M'Naghten rule, a British legal precedent stating that "if the accused knew the nature of his act, and knew it was wrong, then he is mentally competent" (267). Further, as prosecutor Logan Green makes clear, specialized psychiatric testimony is not required since the determination of any family doctor will suffice: "'Medical doctors in general practice. That's all the law requires. We have sanity hearings in this county every year'" (267). This ruling restricts the ground for arguments and limits the jury's view of all potential evidence.

A more distant underpinning of the legal system is the biblical view of crime and punishment, placing the prosecutors in the role of vengeful Old Testament prophets, invoking the *lex talonis*. Prosecutor Green effectively uses a "reading" of biblical passages in his summation to call for the deaths of Hickock and Smith:

> "But I anticipated that defense counsel would use the Holy Bible as an argument against the death penalty. You heard the Bible quoted. But *I* can read too ... and here are a few things that the Good Book has to say on the subject. In Exodus Twenty, Verse Thirteen, we have one of the Ten Commandments: 'Thou shalt not kill' ... [and] in the *next* chapter, Verse Twelve, the penalty for disobedience [is] ... 'He that smiteth a man, so that he die, shall be surely put to death.'" (304)

While the courtroom presentation of evidence focuses on the simple knowledge of right and wrong, Capote undermines the reading of the verdicts by presenting viewpoints of those unsympathetic to the court proceedings. For example, Dick Hickock's father remarks: "'That judge up there! I never seen a man so prejudiced. Just no sense having a trial'" (281). The author also quotes two journalists, who comment on the "cold-blooded" nature of the death penalty. As Capote often stated in interviews, the context and position of quotations help to organize the reader's sense of a scene more effectively than would authorial intrusion. Capote's quotations from the journalists show that "in cold blood" applies first to the killers and then to the state.

While the trial scene is limited by restrictions of the M'Naghten rule to assess sanity, Capote's approach stresses the psychiatric examinations that were inadmissible in court. Since Capote's narrator is unfettered by any legal rulings, he relates the complex theory of Dr. W. Mitchell Jones by stating, "had Dr. Jones been allowed to speak further, here is what he would have said" (294). Jones' assessment of Dick Hickock focuses on his athletic ability and previous good health before a severe auto accident produced "'blackout spells, periods of amnesia and headaches'" (294). He concludes that Hickock's personality has "'typical characteristics of what psychiatrically would be called a severe character disorder,'" and he would have urged the court to order physical examinations to rule out the possibility of "'organic brain damage'" (295). As usual, Capote's lengthier and more penetrating presentation is devoted to psychological evidence concerning Perry Smith's early traumas and his violently explosive behavior.

Dr. Jones finds "'two features in [Smith's] personality make-up stand out as particularly pathological.'" The first is a paranoid orientation toward social interactions: "'He is suspicious and distrustful of others, tends to feel others ... are unfair to him and do not understand him'" (297). Related to this trait, he is "'sensitive to criticism'" and "'cannot tolerate being made fun of'" (297). The second trait, related directly to the Clutter murders, concerns

> "rages, which he says 'mount up' in him, and ... the poor control he has over them. When turned toward himself the anger has precipitated ideas of suicide ... [and, at times] ... his thinking [is] ... lost in detail, and some of his thinking reflects a 'magical' quality, a disregard of reality." (297)

In addition to Dr. Jones' conclusions, Capote quotes extensively from a 1960 paper by Dr. Joseph Satten and his three colleagues, "Murder without Apparent Motive—A Study in Personality Disorganization." Studying the Clutter case, Dr. Satten finds that Smith's behavior conforms to a pattern of murders he had studied where the murderers suffered from "'severe lapses in ego control,'" leading to "'the open expression of primitive violence, born out of previous, and now unconscious, traumatic experiences'" (298–99). For more than ten pages, Capote presents the behavior pattern of such murderers who, on the surface, "'seem rational, coherent, and controlled'" but whose crimes "'have a bizarre, apparently senseless quality'" (298).

At the heart of Dr. Satten's theory is the idea of unconscious motivation, that a present action is determined by the repetition of some earlier, unresolved state of mental imbalance. The murderer in effect finds in the current situation a configuration that provokes a reenactment of old wrongs:

> "Such individuals can be considered murder-prone in the sense of carrying a surcharge of aggressive energy or having an unstable ego defense system that periodically allows the naked and archaic expression of such energy. The murderous potential can become activated, especially if some disequilibrium is already present, when the victim-to-be is unconsciously perceived as a key figure in some past traumatic configuration." (301)

Such parallels reinforce the viewpoint that Dr. Satten "feels secure in assigning [Smith] to 'their ranks'" (301). The proposed theory suggests that Mr. Clutter "was not entirely a flesh-and-blood man [that Smith] 'suddenly discovered' himself destroying" (302) but the cumulative ghost of his father, his despised Army sergeant, the nuns who beat him, and thus all the hated authority figures from his past.

After an extended presentation of these theories, Capote examines Smith's own words, heard earlier both in the confession scene and during a meeting with Don Cullivan, his old Army buddy. In that meeting Smith describes the killing of Mr. Clutter in almost exactly the same words as in the confession scene:

> "I was sore at Dick.... But it wasn't Dick. Or the fear of being identified.... And it wasn't because of anything that the Clutters did. They never hurt me. Like other people. Like people have all my life. Maybe it's just that the Clutters were the ones who had to pay for it." (290)

Capote's narrative voice concludes neutrally by showing the apparent harmony of two viewpoints, reporting that, "It would appear that by independent paths, both the professional and the amateur analyst reached conclusions not dissimilar" (302). Capote's narrator does not interpret these conclusions, but the length of time devoted to them clearly undercuts the straightforward clarity of courtroom justice.

Yet how does the psychiatric testimony work? Although it does not change anything about the laws operating in Kansas in 1960, it questions the fairness of death-penalty verdicts endorsed by the community. Readers must wonder: if Smith underwent a "brain explosion" at the time of murdering

Mr. Clutter, how could he be held responsible? It may seem to be a clear case of temporary insanity. Capote's inherent plea for mercy, however, must later be subjected to cold-blooded facts of the murders of Herbert, Kenyon, Nancy, and Mrs. Clutter. It is clear that they are just as dead whether they were killed by Smith in an agitated state, or because he was intent on leaving no *witnesses* to the crime—a motive for the murders reinforced throughout "The Last to See Them Alive." The weight of the psychiatric testimony does not suggest that Smith and Hickock are *not* guilty, but it hints that leniency or perhaps life imprisonment without parole would be a more suitable punishment, although Capote never overtly makes this argument.

EXECUTION AND FINAL MEANING

The last of the trio of scenes examining the framework of a meaningful design is the execution of Hickock and Smith, depicting events at the Kansas State Penitentiary on April 14, 1965, after five years of legal appeals. As preparation for the events to come, Capote depicts the execution of Lowell Lee Andrews, a Death-Row friend of Hickock and Smith. According to Capote's narrative voice, Smith is allowed to speak a condemned man's customary last words: "'I don't believe in capital punishment, morally or legally. Maybe I had something to contribute, something—'" (340). While journalist Philip Tompkins quotes others close to the scene who stated that these words were not spoken (170), Capote depicts Smith as both penitent and critical of the state. In interviews after the publication of *In Cold Blood*, Capote echoed Smith's own sense of his potential for some future contribution:

> He wanted very deeply to paint and write and he also had genuine talent as a musician. He had a natural ear and could play five or six instruments; the guitar, in particular, he played extremely well. But one of the things he used to tell me over and over again was what a tragedy that ... [no one] encouraged him in any single creative thing he wanted to do. (Norden 125–26)

Yet when Hickock finally dies at 12:41 A.M. and Smith follows at 1:19 A.M., Capote's narrator again turns to Alvin Dewey, the same moral barometer consulted in each phase of the case. Based on comments Dewey no doubt made to Capote, Hickock remains as always "'a smalltime chiseler who got out of his depth'" (340), and yet in death Smith possesses the "aura of an exiled animal, a creature walking wounded" (341). This last description echoes the book's earlier references to Smith's childhood and his wounded adulthood, seen through sympathetic observers like Don Cullivan, Mrs. Josie Meier in Garden City, and his prison friend Willie-Jay.

The closing scene of this nonfiction novel is not the executions proper, since they, once again, fail to provide Alvin Dewey with "a sense of climax, release, of a design justly completed" (341). Capote's language suggests Aristotle's analysis of catharsis in tragedy, in which terror and pity are released in the audience by the appropriate completion of an action at the play's end (*Poetics*, ch. 13–14). In the Clutter case, however, the accidents of a "brain explosion" and the Clutters' accidental presence as victims, as well as Capote's emphasis on the long legal delays, all block the proper purging of the expected emotions at the completion of a well-made plot. Instead, Capote singles out Dewey's memory of a graveside meeting at River Valley Cemetery "a year earlier," a chance encounter with Susan Kidwell, Nancy Clutter's girlhood friend who had gone on to the university to study:

> "Everything Art, mostly. I love it.... Nancy and I planned to go to college together. We were going to be roommates. I think about it sometimes. Suddenly, when I'm very happy, I think of all the plans we made." (342)

After a brief discussion of Nancy's former boyfriend's marriage, and of her own plans, Dewey acknowledges "a pretty girl in a hurry" and he privately thinks she is "just such a young woman as Nancy might have been" (343). The scene nostalgically closes with a sense of place that recalls Capote's *The Grass Harp*, when Collin Fenwick is reunited with Judge Cool. Here Dewey is walking home "leaving behind him the big sky, the whisper of wind voices in the wind-bent wheat" (343). At first this scene seems a fitting way to end, something out of the world of fiction. Yet it also presents a cliché in response to death, asserting the old truism that "life goes on" while survivors must resolve their own searches for meaning.

This ending's strong sense of closure has seemed to certain critics to be tacked on artificially (Tanner 101–2; Macdonald 48). Apparently, Capote did not want to end on the downbeat note of the executions, which were very troubling to him after five years of close contact with the killers. Gerald Clarke's biography asserts that Capote *invented* this graveside scene. *In Cold Blood's* "one act of pure fiction," was revealed as such a decade after the book's publication in a letter from Sue Kidwell's mother and Alvin Dewey (Clarke 358–59; n. 585). This is a serious blemish on the otherwise factually accurate narrative; as Clarke notes, "since events had not provided him with a happy scene, he was forced to make one up" (358–59). Despite this problem of accuracy, does Capote's concluding fiction really imply that the world is restored to order, that a rational structure has been superimposed on the baffling events? Or does the scene function as a kind of musical coda that extends or modifies the formal ending as in a symphonic movement?

In closing this discussion, I want to return once again to the standard of meaningful design to assess its influence on our final interpretation of *In Cold Blood*. Despite the sense of closure Capote's invented ending implies, the book does not really resolve the conflicted meanings of the crimes or bring them within a larger framework that is rationalized, totalized, and complete. A strong reading of this sort is proposed by Phyllis Frus in her recent comparison of *In Cold Blood* with Norman Mailer's *The Executioner's Song*. She argues that Capote's novel reinforces standard class ideology by achieving a defined sense of resolution:

> The narrative of *In Cold Blood* implies that truth is, if not simple, at least ascertainable, if we are willing to take the trouble; and that sociologists and psychiatrists have the answers to the riddle of criminal behavior. Furthermore, the reader implied by the structure of the novel learns that violent, senseless crime can be made sensible and poignant through artistic representation; and that these repulsive, illiterate, antisocial criminals are rendered as literate, talented, redeemable.... *In Cold Blood* ... assumes a world of cause and effect, of certitude, reason—in short, of common sense, and it expresses this world view via a realism characterized by verisimilitude, a historical narrator who assures the intelligibility of the text by "placing" the other narrations, and through its strong sense of closure. (184)

While this reading of closure and certainty of *In Cold Blood* raises many interesting problems, it is ultimately reductive and mistaken in terms of Capote's complex narrative strategies. Although Dewey's category of "meaningful design" is three times raised by the narrator as a possible standard for resolution, nowhere is it accepted or fully endorsed. Furthermore, while the psychiatric testimony is "placed" in an important position in "The Corner," it is never accepted as the final answer to the "riddle of criminal behavior"; in fact, it is only one part of the explanatory apparatus of the narration, since the law and legal proceedings have their due, along with the desire for retribution of the people of Holcomb. I would argue that Capote's structure places the reader in a complex intersection of the law, the impulse for compassion, and the knowledge of psychiatry without fully endorsing a single, stable viewpoint naturalized by "common sense" or reason.

Chris Anderson explains that the mystery of murder in *In Cold Blood* is presented through what he calls a "rhetoric of silence." In effect, Capote's reluctance to impose meaning produces an uncertain ending, one that reproduces our uncertainty when "the imagination fails to comprehend the quality and degree of suffering the Clutters endured" (Anderson 84). In fact, the moment of cutting Mr. Clutter's throat is portrayed as silent and inexplicable because "in the end things just happened; at the key moment there is a blank" (Anderson 64). It is this blank—a moment that resists reduction to language—which the whole trial scene and Smith's confessional account do not domesticate or tame by reason. The events at the center of the murders, despite the full psychological backgrounds and the lengthy confessional statements, produce a reverberation of many texts resounding, while the narrator of *In Cold Blood* declines to single out any explanatory framework as superior or definitive.

With respect to the psychiatric testimony, despite its strong placement, the reader realizes in a way that Frus seems not to accept that psychiatric knowledge will not clear away the mystery of the case. Such thinking is a kind of trap, for, as Alan Dershowitz has recently pointed out in *The Abuse Excuse*, what murderer could not claim an abused childhood or environmental preconditions for murder? At the closing of *In Cold Blood*, Capote positions the reader within a competition of explanatory and rational texts without endorsing any of them and without reducing the mysteries of the case to common wisdom.

What Anderson calls "the rhetoric of silence" implies a narrator who places us in the midst of these explanatory systems, leaving a troubling series of thoughts but never leading to any easy resolution. Are these men guilty? Certainly, on the basis of the evidence at trial, most would say "yes." Are they insane? According to the M'Naghten rule they are sane, yet the psychiatric testimony makes childhood abuse and possible brain damage from motor accidents challenge this ruling. Should Smith's painting and studying of philosophy on Death Row be taken into account? Does journal-keeping indicate that Hickock and Smith are redeemable? "Yes," some might say again. Yet Capote leaves readers with an unwieldy series of accidents, as Conniff points out, brought about by real events: the pairing of these two partners, the particular set of American values the Clutters seem to represent, the feelings that Smith experiences at the precise moment of being poised with a knife above Mr. Clutter's throat. What remains is an irreducible blank and a mystery at the center not unlike Kurtz's cry, "the horror, the horror" in *Heart of Darkness*. None of this can easily be paraphrased.

Finally, do readers accept the town's need for revenge, supported by a biblical call for justice, or the chief detective's need to feel an appropriate set of emotions to achieve a personal closure? Even if they do, there are the dangers of accepting the potentially exculpatory evidence of psychiatry that might eventually lead to self-less agents lost in a world of post-Freudian determinism. *In Cold Blood*, despite its authorial omniscience and its apparent sense of closure, requires acceptance of no particular viewpoint without the simultaneous consideration of other powerful and contradictory explanations. At the end of an interview—published in the *New York Times Book Review*—Capote was asked if he personally had achieved a sense of closure with the case and he replied: "It's like the echo of E. M. Forster's Malabar Caves, the echo that's meaningless and yet it's there: one keeps hearing it all the time" (Plimpton 68). It is perhaps this memory of the vertigo beyond language that he hoped to reproduce for readers of *In Cold Blood*.

NOTE

1. Numerous post-structuralist theorists have explored the relationship between social reality and language. Foremost among these is Michel Foucault who, in such works as "The Discourse on Language," *Discipline and Punish*, and *The History of Sexuality, Volume I: An Introduction*, examines the relationship between knowledge and power in social institutions such as the clinic, the prison system, and the social control of sexuality. A key tenet in this analysis is that reality does not exist independently of the language and discursive practices of social institutions that are shaped by them. In Capote's work, the narrative method heightens the sense of the tension between punishing and vengeful language (exhibited by prosecutors) and the therapeutic language of psychology (exhibited by the defense). Capote thereby positions the implied reader of *In Cold Blood* between these competing ways of conceiving of crime and criminality leading to ambiguous results.

WORKS CITED

Anderson, Chris. *Style as Argument*. Carbondale: Southern Illinois University Press, 1987. 48–81.

Aristotle. *The Rhetoric and Poetics*. Trans. Ingram Bywater. New York: Modern Library, 1954.

Capote, Truman. *In Cold Blood*. New York: Random House, 1965.

Clarke, Gerald. *Truman Capote: A Biography*. New York: Simon and Schuster, 1988.

Conniff, Brian. "Psychological Accidents: 'In Cold Blood' and Ritual Sacrifice." *Midwest Quarterly* 35 (Autumn 1993): 77–94.

Foucault, Michel. *Discipline and Punish: The Birth of the Prison*. Trans. A. M. Sheridan Smith. New York: Harper, 1972.

———. "The Discourse on Language." *The Archaeology of Knowledge*. Trans. A. M. Sheridan Smith. New York: Harper, 1976. 215–37.

———. *The History of Sexuality, Volume 1: An Introduction*. Trans. Robert Hurley. New York: Pantheon, 1978.

Frus, Phyllis. *The Politics and Poetics of Journalistic Narrative*. Cambridge: Cambridge University Press, 1994. 120–56.

Inge, Thomas M., ed. *Truman Capote: Conversations*. Jackson and London: University of Mississippi Press, 1987.

Macdonald, Dwight. "Cosa Nostra." *Esquire* (April 1966): 44+.

Norden, Eric. "Playboy Interview: Truman Capote." *Playboy* (March 1968); rpt. Inge: 110–63.

Plimpton, George. "The Story Behind a Nonfiction Novel." *New York Times Book Review*, 16 January 1966, 2+; rpt in Inge: 47–68.

Tanner, Tony. "Death in Kansas." *Spectator* (18 March 1966): 331–32.

Tompkins, Philip K. "In Cold Fact." *Esquire* (June 1966): 125+.

Trilling, Diana. "Capote's Crime and Punishment." *Partisan Review* (Spring 1966): 252–59. Rpt. *Truman Capote's 'In Cold Blood': A Critical Handbook*. Ed. Irving Malin. Belmont, Calif.: Wadsworth, 1968. 107–13.

Wolfe, Tom, and E. W. Johnson, eds. *The New Journalism, with an Anthology Edited by Tom Wolfe and E. W. Johnson*. New York: Harper & Row, 1973.

WILLIAM WHITE TISON PUGH

Boundless Hearts in a Nightmare World: Queer Sentimentalism and Southern Gothicism in Truman Capote's Other Voices, Other Rooms

In the 1941 article, "the gothic south," Louise Bogan declares, "The definite Gothic quality which characterizes so much of the work of writers from the American South has puzzled critics."[1] In addition to puzzling the critics, however, the ascription of the Southern gothic label to their writings has often puzzled, if not insulted, the Southern writers themselves. In response to Alice Walker's question whether she had ever been called a gothic writer, Eudora Welty replied, "They better not call me that! Yes, I have been, though. Inevitably, because I'm a Southerner. I've never had anybody call me that to my face."[2] Though perhaps not taking such offense at the ascription of a gothic style, Flannery O'Connor likewise believed that some critics both too quickly link the Southern with the gothic and apply the term grotesque to Southern literature when it is not appropriate: she humorously commented that "I have found that anything that comes out of the South is going to be called grotesque by the Northern reader, unless it is grotesque, in which case it is going to be called realistic."[3] Paradoxically, a review of the critical literature about these authors and other Southern writers confirms Bogan's characterization of the literature rather than Welty's and O'Connor's. The assumption of a Southern gothic style is virtually the *sine qua non* of a critical analysis of Southern literature.[4]

From *The Mississippi Quarterly* 51, no. 4 (Fall 1998). © 1999 by Mississippi State University.

Another author who has often been dubbed a Southern gothicist is Truman Capote. Reading his *Other Voices, Other Rooms* in opposition to this background of grotesque critical interpretation,[5] I believe, offers an alternate reading of the novel in which certain characters are not interpreted merely as freakish aberrations and grotesque incarnations but as poignant and sympathetic representations of humanity. My goal is to liberate the text from a reductive critical past in order to begin a process of reinterpretation both of Capote's novel and of other Southern writings which have been too casually labeled "gothic" without sufficient analysis of how the gothic tropes interplay with other literary traditions. Specifically, I argue that Capote employs gothicism in tandem with sentimentalism. Though the gothic and the sentimental may appear to be radically discrete literary traditions, Capote merges them to great effect in *Other Voices, Other Rooms* both to create a hybrid style of gothic sentimentalism in which gothic terror and sentimental pathos combine to solicit the reader's sympathy for the characters, and to bring out the theme that love in any form must be cherished.[6] More specifically, one can see that Capote has created a sentimental novel designed to bring his readers into a sympathetic relationship with the protagonist as this character moves through the nightmare world in which he lives and learns, by so doing, to accept his homosexuality. Rather than merely offering a parade of grotesques and freaks to shock the reader, the didactically sentimental thematics of *Other Voices, Other Rooms* urge the novel's audience to a better understanding and deeper acceptance of homosexuality through a groundbreaking treatment of adolescent gay identity.

THE GOTHIC ELEMENTS

Certainly, I do not want to minimize the gothic elements of the text in my argument that Capote is writing within the sentimental tradition. For example, the landscape of *Other Voices, Other Rooms* is indeed fully gothic in its terror. Capote isolates his characters in the principal setting of the novel, a secluded Southern mansion, and the name of this ancestral manor, Skully's Landing, is itself evocative of death, bones, and decay. The novel begins with the adolescent protagonist, Joel Harrison Knox, traveling from New Orleans to the Landing in order to live with his father after his mother's death, and the descriptions of the landscape through which he travels foreshadow the deterioration which he finds upon his arrival: Capote describes the swamp lands which Joel passes through as "filled with luminous green logs that shine under the dark marsh water like drowned corpses."[7] The boy is then stranded in Sydney Katz's "gloomy café" (p. 12) until Sam Radclif drives him farther; the toy skull on Radclif's gear shift foreshadows Joel's destination, Skully's Landing, which the local townspeople refer to as "The Skulls" (p. 30). In numerous other passages of the book, Capote establishes the foreboding setting of the novel with key elements of the gothic tradition, such as ghostly presences (the mysterious woman in the window), supernatural tales (the local folklore surrounding the Cloud Hotel), and surreal dreams (Joel's delusions during his sickness).

Capote further connects the moldering landscape of Skully's Landing to gothic tropes through the piercing loneliness which plagues the characters who inhabit it; the descriptions of Joel's journey emphasize that he is traveling through "lonesome country" (p. 9). The end of his journey offers no respite to the piercing isolation Joel feels as Zoo, the housekeeper of the Landing, declares that "you ain't got no notion what lonesome is till you stayed a spell at the Landin'" (p. 61). Isolation is a key trope of the gothic novel because the characters must be removed from the safety and comfort offered by other people; as Irving Malin notes, the "Gothic employs a microcosm ... [such as] Skully's Landing ... [in which] there is enough room for irrational (and universal) forces to explode."[8] Certainly, the gothic setting of *Other Voices, Other Rooms* fits this description in its closed atmosphere in which gloom, skulls, and loneliness are Joel's only companions.

READING CHARACTERS SENTIMENTALLY

Though the setting and the atmosphere of the novel are indeed gothic, critics have been too quick to assume that a gothic setting necessitates that *all* of the characters be grotesques. For example, John W. Aldridge describes four of the primary personalities of the novel—Joel, Idabel Thompkins, Cousin Randolph, and Mr. Sansom—as "superbly and grotesquely effective in themselves [though they] illuminate nothing beyond themselves" (p. 202). Bruce Bawer mentions the "Southern Gothic touches" of the novel which include "grotesque characters [and] haunting scenes" (p. 39), but he does not elaborate upon why he views the characters in this way or detail specifically which of the characters are grotesques. William Nance, in a description of Zoo, writes that "she is also, *like everyone at the Landing* ... a grotesque."[9] I agree with Nance that Zoo is a grotesque figure, for Capote describes her as "almost a freak, a human giraffe (p. 59)[10]; however, Nance does not elucidate why Joel, Cousin Randolph, Amy, and Ed Sansom should be considered grotesques. These critics see *all* of the novel's characters as equally grotesque inhabitants of a darkly gothic world; nevertheless, though they decry the "grotesque" characters of the novel over and over, they do not specify why these characters should be read as grotesques. The question then arises whether all of the characters should be interpreted as grotesques or if an alternate interpretation exists. I contend that we must look both to the gothic and to the sentimental traditions to understand how Capote constructs certain characters as grotesques while others are representatives of an affective sentimentality.

In *To Kiss the Chastening Rod*, G. M. Goshgarian outlines the basic tropes and themes of the sentimental novel, and their presence in *Other Voices, Other Rooms* supports my argument that the gothic elements of the text are working in conjunction with the sentimental. Goshgarian declares that writers of sentimental literature

> focus on middle-class home life; appeal massively to their readers' tenderest emotions; deal in types rather than psychologically individuated characters; write with evangelical ends in mind; and compulsively chronicle the improbable career of a pious, nubile, aboriginally middle-class but temporarily déclassée white American girl whose exemplary fortitude under a storm of adversities is rewarded with a spouse, solvency, and salvation. (p. 9)

With only minor modifications, all five of Goshgarian's parameters of sentimental literature appear in Capote's novel: (1) The deteriorating condition of Skully's Landing indicates that Randolph's financial situation has declined from its past heights and, thus, that the novel's setting is not in the upper class but in the middle; (2) Capote makes outright demands upon the reader's emotions and models the appropriate sympathetic responses to his characters; (3) certain characters are introduced as types rather than as fully fleshed individuals in order to accentuate their sentimental appeal; (4) though Capote does not write with evangelical objectives, he does write didactically in order to lead his readers to a better acceptance of homosexuality; (5) and Joel, forced out into the world after his mother's death, is an adolescent gay male version of the typically feminine sentimental protagonist as he withstands the onslaught of adversity and emerges with a partner (though "solvency and salvation" are not addressed in the text) through his relationship with Randolph at the novel's end. Moreover, Capote's revisions of the fourth and fifth tropes—metamorphosing evangelical objectives into a didactic appeal to accept sexual-orientation difference and replacing a heterosexual female heroine with a gay adolescent hero—suggest that the sentimentalism at the heart of his project has specifically queer objectives, and I therefore refer to Capote's sentimentalism as a queer sentimentalism. A middle-class setting, claims on the reader's sympathy, stock characters, didactic appeals, and the protagonist's perseverance in the face of overwhelming odds—all of these elements of the sentimental tradition are included in *Other Voices, Other Rooms*. With so much queer sentimentalism, why, then, should all of the characters be read as grotesques? And which of the characters should be read sentimentally?

Other than the invalid Mr. Sansom, the chief mark of difference for the characters that Aldridge labels grotesques is their respective sexual ambiguities, as Joel is a "sissy," Idabel is a tomboy, and Cousin Randolph is effeminate. The many descriptions of these characters throughout the novel underscore that they do not adhere to traditional gender roles: Joel is "too pretty, too delicate and fair-skinned, each of his features was shaped with a sensitive accuracy, and a girlish tenderness softened his eyes, which were brown and very large" (p. 11); Capote's portrait of Idabel emphasizes her masculine manners and her rough-and-tumble ways, evident in her male attire ("a pair of brown shorts and a yellow polo shirt") and her rambunctious antics ("Whooping like a wildwest Indian, the redhead whipped down the road" [p. 26]); Randolph's defining characteristics are his smoothness and his femininity, as his face "was round as a coin, smooth and hairless; ... curly, very blond, his fine hair fell in childish yellow ringlets across his forehead, and his wide-set womanly eyes were sky-blue marbles" (p. 84). These descriptions certainly set the characters apart from heterosexuality, but they do not construct them as grotesques. Thus, because Aldridge and other critics do not specify why these characters should be read as grotesques, I surmise that their indictments of the characters are based upon both the characters' location in a gothic setting and the heterosexist labeling both of sexual-orientation difference and of gender cross-over as grotesque. Certainly, a good deal of the criticism of *Other Voices, Other Rooms* is explicitly homophobic: the reviewer of the novel for *Time* magazine declared that "the distasteful trappings of its homosexual theme overhang it like Spanish moss."[11] This and other unsympathetic critical reactions mirror the responses of many homophobic characters in the novel to those who do not adhere to traditional gender mores, as when, for example, the wife of the one-armed barber declares that "it wasn't no revelation to me cause I always knew *she was a freak*, no ma'am, never saw Idabel Thompkins in a dress yet" (p. 27; emphasis added). With critics unsympathetic to the homosexuality of the story, that Joel, Idabel, and Randolph have been read as freakish aberrations rather than as sentimental tropes refashioned from a queer perspective should come as no surprise.

Indeed, Capote shows that such closed-minded opinions have been successful to a degree in convincing the gay and lesbian characters themselves that they are grotesques. In the account of his experiences with Ed Sansom, Dolores, and Pepe, Cousin Randolph refers to his friends and himself as "grotesque quadruplets" (p. 153); however, Miss Wisteria, the dwarf in the carnival with whom Idabel later falls in love, explicitly counters this view and emphasizes that the gay and lesbian characters are not grotesques, though even they themselves may think they are freaks because of society's reaction to them. In her sympathetic encounter with Idabel, Miss Wisteria brings to light the damage which the townspeople have done to the adolescent girl when she rhetorically asks, "Poor child, is it that she believes she is a freak, too?" (p. 199). Miss Wisteria's question demonstrates her understanding that Idabel may believe herself grotesque because of the constant abuse she receives from both the townspeople and her family; nevertheless, Miss Wisteria's compassionate concern also clearly demonstrates that Idabel is not a freak but a human being who has for too long been subjected to inhumane treatment by those around her. Joel, Idabel, and Randolph are viewed as grotesques only through closed-minded misperceptions; Capote ensures that their humanity and pain are always at the forefront of the novel so that the reader is forced to confront the results of such barbarity. And it is superbly appropriate that Capote allows Miss Wisteria, who in other novels would be immediately recognizable as a grotesque character because of her dwarfism, to be the voice of this concern, as this allows a traditionally grotesque figure the symbolic opportunity to reclaim herself from misreadings. Furthermore, Capote highlights the ironic hypocrisy of the townspeople who label these characters as grotesques because the townspeople themselves are directly linked to the gothic tradition through their own grotesque features: the one-armed barber suffers an obvious physical absence; the simian Miss Roberta has "long ape-like arms that were covered with dark fuzz, and there was a wart on her chin, and decorating this wart was a single antenna-like hair" (p. 28); the avian Florabel becomes an odd parody of the model of propriety she believes herself to be, as "she talked rapidly in a flighty, too birdlike manner, as if mimicking a certain type of old lady" (p. 37).

When the gay and lesbian characters of *Other Voices, Other Rooms* are viewed as tropes of the sentimental tradition, the flatness which some critics observe becomes a necessary marker of a specific literary genre. Janet Todd, in providing an overview of the elements of the sentimental, declares that "the arousal of pathos through conventional situations, *stock familial characters* and rhetorical devices is the mark of sentimental literature."[12] Todd furthermore affirms the sentimental's need for characters who are "distressed [and] natural victims, whose misery is demanded by their predicament as defenceless women, aged men, helpless infants or melancholic youths" (p. 3). Interestingly, of the four characters of the novel whom Aldridge addresses, three specifically belong to the categories of sentimental characters which Todd delineates: Joel and Idabel are both "melancholic youths" and Mr. Sansom is an "aged man" and hopeless invalid. Craig M. Goad, though not specifically recognizing the characters' debt to the sentimental tradition, points out the symbolic nature of the text's personae:

> Joel is not a normal member of any normal society, but rather a symbol of everyone who struggles against overwhelming odds to establish an identity and to find love.... None of these characters, despite their lovable natures, is, properly speaking, a person. They represent abstract qualities of non-conformity, charity, understanding and other virtues. They exist, not as people, but as representations of the way people ought to be if only the world would let them be so. (p. 13)

Within a queer sentimental interpretation, Joel, Idabel, and Randolph can be read not as grotesques, but as character types integrally designed to elicit a sympathetic response from the reader.

The novel's sympathetic and sentimental tropes stress the humanity of the homosexual characters, a humanity which Capote does not allow to be stripped from them. Rather, he often stresses the appropriate emotional responses to his characters, as when, for example, Idabel laments to Joel the problems of being a girl:

> "I never think like I'm a girl; you've got to remember that, or we can't never be friends." For all its bravado, she made this declaration with a special and compelling innocence; and when she knocked one fist against the other, as, frowning, she did now, and said: "I want so much to be a boy: I would be a sailor, I would ..." *the quality of her futility was touching.* (p. 136, emphasis added)

Capote directs the reader's response, ordering the audience to be "touched" by Idabel's plight, to understand the pain which gender codes have placed upon her. Capote employs his stock characters of the little boy lost (Joel), the tomboy (Idabel), and the loveless lonely-heart (Randolph) to guide his readers into a sympathetic relationship with them.

In *Sentimental Modernism*, Suzanne Clark declares that "tropes of sympathy argue through embodiment and an appeal to experience: the sentimental locates moral values in the (feminized) heart and denies the importance of external differences. Thus the sentimental also grounds the moral appeal to respect individual differences" (p. 22). In this light, Capote's didactic aims are apparent: the depiction of these unique characters is intended to initiate a relationship between reader and character in which the former learns to respect the latter. The difference and otherness of Joel, Idabel, and Randolph is located in their refusal of a socially assigned heterosexuality; the thematic thrust of *Other Voices, Other Rooms* seeks to bring its readers to an acceptance of homosexuality through a sympathetic relationship with its characters. Moreover, I find this didacticism to be part of the novel's sentimental, rather than its gothic, tradition. Though gothic literature may also be didactic, gothic didacticism is not predicated upon the reader's sympathetic relationship with the characters. For example, Flannery O'Connor is outrightly didactic in such short stories as "A Good Man is Hard to Find" and "Good Country People," but the moral lesson does not derive from our sympathy for such characters as the Grandmother or Joy "Hulga" Hopewell; rather, we are invited to laugh at them as we learn O'Connor's moral thematics. The didacticism of *Other Voices, Other Rooms*, however, is based upon our heartfelt sympathies for the gay and lesbian characters. Gothic didacticism may function despite an affective separation between reader and character(s); sentimental didacticism depends upon the reader's emotional cathexis with the character(s).

Boundless Hearts in a Nightmare World

Within the first few pages of the text, Capote arouses the reader's sympathy for Joel both through the many hardships and losses the boy has endured and through his effeminate character, which marks him as an outsider to the heteronormative world outside Skully's Landing. His mother has recently died from pneumonia, and he feels isolated from everyone else in the world; when he imagines himself trapped in a frozen palace, he asks himself, "What living soul would then brave robber barons for his rescue?" and concludes that "there was no one, really no one" (p. 17). Joel's isolation in his past life is mirrored by his sense of abandonment in his present: upon arriving at a town close to Noon City, he cannot finish his journey because, as he says, "no one come to meet me" (p. 11). Even the conclusion of Joel's travels will not end the solitude thrust upon him since his mother's death because Joel has never met his father: "'I've never seen him,' said Joel" (p. 15). The pathos of a little boy lost immediately demands the reader's heartfelt attention to Joel, as does the effeminacy which marks him as the "Other" to patriarchal society. Capote stresses Joel's separation from a masculine ethos, as Sam Radclif dislikes Joel immediately for his feminine qualities: "Radclif eyed the boy ... not caring much for the looks of him. He had his notions of what a 'real' boy should look like, and this kid somehow offended them" (pp. 10-11). Capote ensures the reader's sympathy for his protagonist by marking him as totally alone in the world; Joel has no one to care for him except the audience of the text. In his little prayer, "Only how, how could you say something so indefinite, so meaningless as this: God, let me be loved" (p. 79), Capote delineates the tragically simple quest of Joel's life.

Capote further emphasizes the chasm between Joel and patriarchy by the differences in Joel's and his father's last names: Joel's mother chose "Knox" for the boy's surname after her divorce from his father, Mr. Sansom. The patronymic difference between Joel and his father stresses Joel's separation from patriarchal codes and marks him as an outsider in a predominantly masculine and heterosexual society, as evidenced by the reaction of Sam Radclif to the boy's last name: "'Aw, say, son' said Radclif, 'you oughtn't to have let [your mother] done that! Remember, your Pa's your Pa no matter what'" (pp. 14-15). Though Joel's surname distances him from the heteronormative community which his father and Radclif represent, Capote also employs Joel's name to foreshadow the boy's rejection of the homophobic society which places such an emphasis on the father's name. Judith Butler concludes in her analysis of the patronym that "patronymic names endure over time, as nominal zones of phallic control. Enduring and viable identity is thus purchased through subjection to and subjectivation by the patronym."[13] Through Joel's rejection of the patronym, Capote points forward to the character's rejection of the social codes which inhibit the development of his homosexuality. Joel's surname is thus a means both to highlight his isolation in and to foreshadow his freedom from the patriarchal parameters which hamper his acceptance of a gay identity.

Having established that Joel's search for love and acceptance is the focus of the novel, Capote develops this theme in the following scene. Before arriving at Skully's Landing, Joel meets Idabel Thompkins, the local tomboy. His desire for friendship with another outsider is evident in his unspoken address to the girl, "Hi Idabel—watchasay Idabel?" The words, however, are never uttered, and Idabel promptly ignores Joel. Though Joel does not connect with Idabel at this point of the narrative, Capote uses the scene effectively to introduce the reader to Idabel's masculine attributes. He writes that "[h]er voice was boy-husky" (p. 31) and depicts Miss Roberta admonishing Idabel both to "learn a few lady-like manners" and to "put on some decent female clothes" (p. 32). Although Joel and Idabel do not meet in this passage, Capote establishes their mutual status as outsiders due to their inabilities to conform to traditional gender roles.

Joel and Idabel become friends in the unfolding of the narrative, but his subsequent relationship with her cannot wholly free him from the isolation he feels. Though Idabel is in many ways Joel's kindred spirit, neither can give the other the love they both need, and, though they attempt to escape together from the world which traps them, they fail because such an escape would not force them to face their respective true identities. Through their ability to make "everything look a lot prettier" (p. 132), Idabel's green-colored glasses symbolize her attempt to make the world more palatable. By changing the world around her with the glasses, Idabel attempts to construct a world which she wants to see. The society in which she and Joel live, however, is not a "pretty" place for the two. Thus, when Joel attempts to kiss Idabel after they have been swimming naked together and, accordingly, to take his place in the heterosexual community, Idabel fights against him and pins him down: "Idabel was astride him, and her strong hands locked his wrists to the ground" (p. 139). In this act of simulated intercourse, as Helen Garson points out, "symbolically the male-female roles are reversed ... Idabel becomes representative of the fierce strength of the conquering male astride the subdued figure of the female" (p. 22). Also important in this scene of reversals is that the green-colored glasses break and cut Joel in his buttocks. Joel's buttocks bear the bloodiness of the loss of virginity which is typically borne on the woman's body in heterosexual intercourse; this inversion of heterosexual bleeding foreshadows his acceptance of homosexuality, in which his virginity is not only marked by his penis but by his anus as well. In the failure of heterosexuality for Joel and Idabel, Capote shows that they cannot escape from their true selves either by an enforced heterosexual union or by the green-colored glasses changing the appearance of the world around them. They must face the struggle to accept themselves, including their homosexuality, despite the society which is unsympathetic to their needs. Green-colored glasses are not sufficient to alter the harsh reality of their lives,[14] and Joel and Idabel must find their identities not by a retreat into heterosexuality but through an acceptance of their homosexuality.

Idabel is the first of the pair successful both in her repudiation of heterosexual norms and in her acceptance of her homosexuality. In a scene which begs for a Freudian interpretation, Idabel and Joel encounter a snake—an obvious metaphor for the phallus—after they have run away from home together. Though Joel is paralyzed with fear and can only see his father in the snake ("How did Mr. Sansom's eyes come to be in a moccasin's head?"), Idabel grabs yet another phallic symbol, Joel's sword, and kills the snake as she calls it a "[b]ig granddaddy bastard" (p. 184). Thus, Idabel is capable of wielding the phallic power of the sword in order to destroy the phallic power of the snake. In her ability to move freely in roles stereotypically associated with the masculine and to eradicate symbolically the constraining influence of the phallus, Idabel liberates herself from patriarchal codes which attempt to restrict her from experiencing her homosexuality. In this newfound freedom, Idabel is able to accept her homosexuality, and she falls in love with Miss Wisteria at the carnival: "[A] queer thing happened ... as [Idabel] continued to fawn over tiny yellow-haired Miss Wisteria it came to [Joel] that Idabel was in love" (p. 197). Joel sees that queer things and queer feelings can happen through Idabel's love for Miss Wisteria, even though the dwarf does not return the young girl's affection. Because Idabel has learned to accept herself and her emotions, Joel is able to comprehend the possibility of accepting his homosexuality.

Cousin Randolph is equally important to Joel in his realization and acceptance of his homosexuality, and Capote's depiction of Randolph similarly ensures that the character be read sympathetically. Before Randolph establishes his residence at the Landing, he has a relationship with Dolores, who introduces him to the man, Pepe, with whom he falls hopelessly in love. Though Randolph has not realized his homosexuality prior to Pepe's arrival, Dolores has deduced the truth and advises Randolph to stay away from Pepe: "'Strange how long it takes us to discover ourselves; I've known since first I saw you,' she said, adding, 'I do not think, though, that he is the one for you; I've known too many Pepes; love him if you will, it will come to nothing'" (p. 151). Dolores's conjecture proves true, and Pepe leaves Randolph. Consequently, Randolph retreats to the Landing where he attempts to regain Pepe's love by writing to him in care of postmasters throughout the world:

> "Over there," said Randolph with a tired smile, "is a five-pound volume listing every town and hamlet on the globe; it is what I believe in, this almanac; day by day I've gone through it writing Pepe always in care of the postmaster; just notes, nothing but my

name and what we will for convenience call address. Oh, I know
that I shall never have an answer. But it gives me something to
believe in. And that is peace." (p. 158)

In this hyperbolic description of the extents to which Randolph will go to
find Pepe, Capote illustrates a heart hungering for the love it craves.
Speaking for all of humanity, Randolph claims that "What we most want is
only to be held ... and told ... that everything ... is going to be all right" (p.
152); the reader cannot help but wish that everything will be all right for him
after following his tragic search for love.

As the novel closes, Joel and Randolph enter into a symbiotic
relationship in which Randolph helps Joel to accept his homosexuality, and
Joel helps to convince Randolph that, indeed, everything will be all right.
After their trip together to the Cloud Hotel, Joel enters Skully's Landing
while Randolph, dressed in drag, waves to him from the window, suggesting
that the two are prepared to begin their new lives together, and will be able
to support each other despite the outside world's disapproving view of their
sexual orientations. Many critics have expressed negative reactions to the
ending of *Other Voices, Other Rooms* because they presume that it suggests a
predatory and dysfunctional sexual relationship between Randolph and Joel
in which the former has molded the latter into a sexual toy and that a
romance ensues with complicated inversions of traditional family
relationships. Goad suggests that "with Joel's rejection of both his father and
male-female sexuality, Randolph is ready to assume the dual role of father
and lover" (p. 30). Marvin Mengeling, in an Oedipal interpretation, declares
that "Joel, therefore, must somehow be infused with the psychological
strength necessary for him to assume the position of husband, not child, in
relation to Randolph, the mother image."[15] Paul Levine suggests that "Joel,
like Christ, is condemned and abandoned by his father and crucified by
surrendering to Randolph" (p. 614). These opinions, and others like them,
assume that gay relationships are predicated upon inversions of traditional
family structures in which one man loves another who fulfills the role of his
parent. I offer an interpretation of the novel's denouement in which
Randolph does not act as Joel's mother, father, or crucifier: Because
Randolph dresses in drag does not mean that Joel wants to sleep with his
mother; because Randolph is older than Joel does not mean that Joel wants
to sleep with his father: because two men share a sexual relationship does not
necessitate that one be crucified. Importantly, too, critics have attacked the
sentimentality of the novel's close: Claude Summers considers that the
ending "represent[s] an escape from reality into the make-believe of

Randolph's sentimental and self-indulgent fantasies."[16] How does the novel's resolution appear when we read it sentimentally, when we interpret a loving relationship rather than a predatory one?

A SENTIMENTAL ENDING

Interpretations which suggest a dysfunctional relationship between Joel and Randolph may be predicated upon Joel's desire to leave Skully's Landing and, thus, to escape from his homosexuality. That Joel wants to escape from homosexuality should not be read as a condemnation of homosexuality; rather, Joel's reluctance to accept his homosexuality serves a key role in his development. Growing up in a homophobic society is intrinsically difficult, and Capote's novel would lack depth if he glossed over this central conflict of Joel's maturation. Thus, Capote describes Joel as desperate to leave the Landing and to return to his home in New Orleans with his Aunt Ellen: "[T]he good feeling came back: Ellen would make things different, she would fix it so he could go away to a school where everybody was like everybody else" (p. 114). Joel, however, can never be "like everybody else" because of his homosexuality, and the acceptance of his gay identity must therefore take place in a setting which will nurture his unique person. The world outside Skully's Landing is wholly inappropriate and hostile to this task. Joel's denial of his homosexuality involves his attempt to run from Skully's Landing; conversely, his acceptance of homosexuality is evident at the end of the novel when he enters the mansion.

The scene in which Randolph leaves with Joel for the Cloud Hotel at the time when Aunt Ellen comes to take him to New Orleans, therefore, should not be interpreted as depicting a cruel homosexual seducer kidnapping a young boy from his loving family. Significantly, Randolph and Joel travel to the Cloud Hotel after Joel's long sickness during which Randolph nurtures him back to health, and, thus, their relationship becomes firmly established. Randolph and he are free to return to their home at Skully's Landing where homosocial and/or homosexual bonds may be forged, and Randolph's presence ensures that Joel will be able to experience his rebirth as a gay man in a gay community rather than retreating into a state of perpetual pre-adolescence in a society which will never understand him. A character who acts as such an exemplar of proper behavior is another marker of the sentimental tradition: Jane Tompkins notes that sentimental novels "always involve, prominently, a mentor-figure who initiates the pupil into the mysteries of the art, and enunciates the values the narrative is attempting to enforce" (p. 176). Is Cousin Randolph serving narratively in such a mentoring fashion?

Randolph's many didactic discourses about love certainly teach Joel how to deal with the emotions he is experiencing at this time of his maturation. Capote describes Joel's benefitting from Randolph's instruction as the boy approaches a fundamental change in which his old self is dead, replaced by the vibrancy of his new identity:

> Now at thirteen Joel was nearer a knowledge of death than in any year to come: a flower was blooming inside him, and soon, when all tight leaves unfurled, when the noon of youth burned whitest, he would turn and look, as others had, for the opening of another door. (p. 131)

Randolph, of course, represents the "others" mentioned in the quotation; as Joel "opens the door" to his homosexuality, so central to the titular thematics of *Other Voices, Other Rooms*, Randolph serves as a mentor for Joel's new self who can now accept and cherish his homosexuality. Indeed, the postcard from Idabel which Randolph burns as Joel convalesces from his illness is further evidence of the distinction between the Joel of the past and the new Joel who has experienced this rebirth; Idabel now is one "whose names concerned the old Joel" (p. 214). Joel's past, including both the good and the bad memories, is sacrificed to his new identity as he thematically opens the door to another room and another life. His quest for his homosexual self has been the overriding focus of the narrative; Randolph, in his exemplary role, assists Joel in the task of finding himself through his gay identity. Though in the novel's opening Joel feels as if he has no identity ("He felt separated, without identity, a stone-boy mounted on the rotted stump" [p. 76]), by the novel's close, Joel is able to proclaim, "I am me, ... I am Joel, we are the same people" (p. 230). In accord, the narrator relates that Joel "knew who he was, he knew that he was strong" (p. 231).[17]

In the closing lines of the text, Capote depicts Joel's acceptance of his homosexuality as the adolescent realizes both that Randolph is the mysterious woman in the window and that his own life will change irrevocably with the acceptance of his new gay identity:

> She [Randolph] beckoned to him, shining and silver, and he knew he must go: unafraid, not hesitating, he paused only at the garden's edge where, as though he'd forgotten something, he stopped and looked back at the bloomless, descending blue, at the boy he had left behind. (p. 235)

Joel moves to enter Skully's Landing at the novel's end, but he and Randolph are not portrayed together as lovers at the novel's end; consequently, we can only hypothesize that they engage in a sexual relationship. Nonetheless, if we assume if the two do engage in a sexual relationship in their seclusion at Skully's Landing, I maintain that the paradigm of this union would not be an inversion of traditional family structures in which Joel partners with Randolph acting either as his mother-or father-figure; rather, Capote asserts throughout the text that the two are equals, nearly mirror images of each other. When Joel first sees Randolph as the mysterious woman, he recognizes aspects of himself: "the hazy substance of her face, the suffused marshmallow features, brought to mind his own vaporish reflection in the wavy chamber mirror" (p. 71). Later, Joel looks into Randolph's eyes and sees himself reflected: "So he questioned the round innocent eyes, and saw his own boy-face focused as in double camera lenses" (p. 91). Capote accentuates both Randolph's youth and Joel's age so that, despite their age difference, the two appear more as equals. Joel writes to his friend Sammy Silverstein that "Out here a person old as us is a grown-up person" (p. 96)[18]; likewise, Randolph's youthfulness is often highlighted as when, for example, Capote writes "the sudden light flattered [Randolph's] face, made the pink hairless skin more impeccably young" (p. 157) or "[Randolph's] skin seemed translucently pink in the morning light, his round smooth face bizarrely youthful" (p. 172). By stressing the likenesses between the two characters, Capote paints their relationship as sharing a fundamental equality.

Furthermore, I would like to point out that Capote is playing with tropes of Narcissism in his depiction of Joel's and Randolph's relationship. Though homosexuality has often been viewed as an excessive form of self-love, Capote redeems Narcissistic tropes from their traditional allegations of egotism and posits Narcissus as a model of human honesty in amorous concerns. In a defense of self-love, Randolph declares: "I tell you, my dear, Narcissus was no egotist ... he was merely another of us who, in our unshatterable isolation, recognized, on seeing his reflection, the one beautiful comrade, the only inseparable love ... poor Narcissus, possibly the only human who was ever honest on this point" (p. 144). Capote then delineates the perfect Narcissistic equality between the two when Joel falls sick and discusses with Randolph their ages and their relationship:

"Randolph," [Joel] said, "were you ever as young as me?" And Randolph said: "I was never so old." "Randolph," he said, "do you know something? I'm very happy." To which his friend made no reply. The reason for this happiness seemed to be simply that he did not feel unhappy, *rather he knew all through him a kind of balance*. There was so little to cope with. The mist which for him had overhung so much of Randolph's conversation, even that had lifted, at least it was no longer troubling, *for it seemed as though he understood him absolutely*. (p. 212, emphases added)

In their Narcissistic balance, Joel and Randolph are free from society's bigotries and ready to embrace their gay identities. That two gay men choose to live with each other in a secluded setting should not be read as an indictment of homosexuality. The society outside Skully's Landing does not care to understand homosexuality, and the two men therefore make a haven for each other in which they are free to live as the gay men they are. Georges-Michel Sarotte believes the novel's dénouement suggests that "Joel has recognized his inner personality, and the joy he shows seems to indicate that he hopes to make his life a paradise ... Joel's refuge in homosexuality is the only solution to the anxiety plaguing anyone who adopts against his nature the sexual mores of society."[19] Joel and Randolph are safe together in their understanding of each other; they have made a world in which self-expression liberates them from the society which would never understand their feelings of love.

In their freedom from the world's homophobia at the Landing, Joel and Randolph serve for the reader as role models of individuals unwilling to forgo their need for love in order to appease the petty dictates of society. In the novel's ending, Capote's sentimentally didactic goal is explicitly to teach his readers that all human love is beautiful. As Cousin Randolph, in his role as Joel's mentor, declares,

> "The brain may take advice, but not the heart, and love, having no geography, knows no boundaries: weight and sink it deep, no matter, it will rise and find the surface: and why not? any love is natural and beautiful that lies within a person's nature; only hypocrites would hold a man responsible for what he loves, emotional illiterates and those of righteous envy, who, in their agitated concern, mistake so frequently the arrow pointing to heaven for the one that leads to hell." (p. 151)

This passage, which expressly states the theme of the novel and speaks the beauty of boundless loves, models the proper reaction of the novel's audience to the characters and their situations. In both his outright exhortation for acceptance of love in its myriad forms and his condemnation of the hypocritically judgmental, Capote urges the reader to a sympathetic relationship with his characters, a relationship universalized to include all human beings who love in ways not condoned by the greater society.

Although Southern gothicism has long been recognized as a distinct body of American fiction, the time is long past due to reassess this label and the assumptions behind it. Rather than always designating the Southern homosexual character as a fascinating yet grotesque "Other," critics must analyze these characters with the same assumptions of fundamental humanity which heterosexual characters have received since the beginnings of literary criticism. One hopes, therefore, that blanket equations of homosexuality and grotesquerie will finally be eradicated both from criticism and from society itself.[20] Certainly, Capote includes a great deal of grotesquerie in *Other Voices, Other Rooms*, but these gothic tropes serve to highlight the plight of his sentimental gay and lesbian characters, not to construct them as freaks. We must be sure to investigate how gothicism interacts with other literary traditions employed in the delineations of gay and lesbian characters: how, for example, would the works of Carson McCullers, Tennessee Williams, and other Southern writers look to us if we looked for traces of queer sentimentalism in their gothic literatures? If they were viewed as sentimental characters, how would the critical interpretations of Frankie of *The Member of the Wedding* or Brick of *Cat on a Hot Tin Roof* change? Along with both the Southern and the gay characters receiving the sympathetic readings they so strongly deserve, perhaps sentimental literature itself would at long last receive the critical approbation which it for too long has been denied.[21]

NOTES

1. Louise Bogan, "The Gothic South," *Nation*, 153 (1941), 572.

2. Alice Walker, "Eudora Welty: An Interview," in Peggy Whitman Prenshaw, ed., *Conversations with Eudora Welty* (Jackson: University Press of Mississippi, 1984), p. 137.

3. Flannery O'Connor, *Mystery and Manners: Occasional Prose*, ed. Sally and Robert Fitzgerald (New York: Farrar, Straus and Giroux, 1969), p. 40.

4. Some recent criticism on this issue includes Dieter Meindl, *American Fiction and the Metaphysics of the Grotesque* (Columbia: University of Missouri Press, 1996) and Louis Gross, *Redefining the American Gothic* (Ann Arbor: University of Michigan Press, 1989). Given Welty's displeasure with the critical association between her literature and gothic tropes, one might

wonder how she would react to Ruth Weston, *Gothic Tradition and Narrative Techniques in the Fiction of Eudora Welty* (Baton Rouge: Louisiana State University Press, 1994).

5. The assumption of Capote's gothicism is apparent in much of the criticism of his works. See, for example, the books and articles by John W. Aldridge, *After the Lost Generation: A Critical Study of the Writers of Two Wars* (New York: McGraw-Hill, 1951); Bruce Bawer, "Capote's Children," *New Criterion*, 3 (1985), 39-44; Helen S. Garson, *Truman Capote* (New York: Frederick Ungar Publishing, 1980); Craig M. Goad, "Daylight and Darkness, Dream and Delusion: The Works of Truman Capote," *Emporia State Research Studies*, 16 (1967), 5-57; and Paul Levine, "Truman Capote: The Revelation of the Broken Image," *Virginia Quarterly Review*, 34 (1958), 600-617.

6. Though sentimental literature has traditionally been viewed as inferior to other forms of fiction, recent scholarship has begun to reclaim the sentimental as a significant and relevant literary tradition in its own right. For scholarship on sentimental literature, see Jane Tompkins, *Sensational Designs: The Cultural Work of American Fiction, 1790-1840* (New York: Oxford University Press, 1985); Howard Fulweiler, *"Here a Captive Heart Busted": Studies in the Sentimental Journey of Modern Literature* (New York: Fordham University Press, 1993); Suzanne Clark, *Sentimental Modernism: Women Writers and the Revolution of the Word* (Bloomington: Indiana University Press, 1991); G. M. Goshgarian, *To Kiss the Chastening Rod: Domestic Fiction and Sexual Ideology in the American Renaissance* (Ithaca, New York: Cornell University Press, 1992); and Claudia Tate, *Domestic Allegories of Political Desire: The Black Heroine's Text at the Turn of the Century* (New York: Oxford University Press, 1992).

7. Truman Capote, *Other Voices, Other Rooms* (New York: Signet, 1948), p. 9.

8. Irving Malin, *New American Gothic* (Carbondale: Southern Illinois University Press, 1962), p. 5.

9. William L. Nance, *The Worlds of Truman Capote* (New York: Stein & Day, 1970), p. 44, emphasis added.

10. Although Capote clearly labels Zoo a grotesque, she is also linked to the sentimental tradition through the scar on her neck. The scar, a visible reminder of her relationship with the villainous Keg Brown, ensures the reader's sympathy for her. Zoo, thus, is herself an example of the gothic sentimentalism which I find in the novel.

11. "Spare the Laurels," *Time*, March 14, 1949, p. 113.

12. Janet Todd, *Sensibility: An Introduction* (London: Methuen, 1986), p.

2, emphasis added. Although Todd's analysis of the sentimental addresses the tradition's British history, her argument about the stock nature of sentimental characters certainly applies to American sentimentalism as well, as the previous quotation from Goshgarian confirms.

13. Judith Butler, *Bodies That Matter: On the Discursive Limits of "Sex"* (New York: Routledge, 1993), p. 153.

14. Green-colored glasses are a recurring motif in *Other Voices, Other Rooms*, and they repeatedly fail in the characters' attempts to use them to escape into a fantasy world (as when Joel remembers his life with the Kendall family "as if he lived those months wearing a pair of spectacles with green, cracked lenses" [p. 17] or when Idabel wins another pair at the carnival "but too large for her, they kept sliding down her nose" [p. 195]). Capote does not allow his characters to escape from their harsh worlds, but depicts them as learning to face homophobic society.

15. Marvin E. Mengeling, "*Other Voices, Other Rooms*: Oedipus Between the Covers." *American Imago*, 19 (1962), 370.

16. Claude J. Summers, *Gay Fictions: Wilde to Stonewall: Studies in a Male Homosexual Literary Tradition* (New York: Frederick Ungar, 1990), p. 132

17. Randolph's role in Joel's maturation is also evident in Capote's internal parody of the thematics of emotional and psycho-sexual development when the author depicts Joel's thirst for alcohol to mark his new-found maturity. At Miss Roberta's diner, Joel asks for beer and is embarrassed by her reply that she "[c]an't serve no beer to minors, babylove, even if you are a might cute-lookin' fella" (p. 29). Randolph's mentoring role is then evident when, by giving Joel alcohol, he provides the first clue to his position as the boy's mentor, as one who will assist him in his growth to manhood.

18. After writing this letter to Sammy, Joel realizes that "almost all he'd ever written were lies, big lies poured over the paper like a thick syrup" (p. 97). The lies, however, address Joel's fantasy vision of his father; I believe that Joel's thoughts about Randolph and his perceptions of age at Skully's Landing are accurate reflections of his world.

19. George-Michel Sarotte, *Like a Brother, Like a Lover: Male Homosexuality in the American Novel and Theater from Herman Melville to James Baldwin* (New York: Anchor Press, 1978), p. 48.

20. I do not mean to suggest that gay, lesbian, or bisexual characters should never be read as grotesques. Certainly, many authors specifically demand that sexual orientation difference be interpreted as a marker of grotesquerie. I do believe, however, that we must be careful not to make

universal and essentializing connections between homosexual or bisexual characters and Southern gothic conventions.

21. I thank Mary Wood, Louise Westling, Margaret Johnson, and the anonymous readers of the *Mississippi Quarterly* for their helpful suggestions throughout the composition of this essay.

Chronology

1924	Born Truman Streckfus Persons on September 30 in New Orleans, son of Lillie Mae (later Nina) Faulk Persons and Arch Persons.
1927	Sent to live with an elderly uncle and three elderly women in rural Alabama.
1931	Parents divorce.
1932	Mother marries Joseph Capote.
1935	Joseph adopts Truman.
1939	Attends boarding schools in New York; then attends Greenwich High School in Millbrook, Connecticut.
1942	Begins work at *The New Yorker* magazine.
1945–48	Publishes short stories in various magazines. Wins two O. Henry awards. Publishes *Other Voices, Other Rooms* in January 1948.
1949	Publishes *A Tree of Night and Other Stories*.
1950	Publishes *Local Color*.
1951	Publishes *The Grass Harp*.
1952	Theatrical version of *The Grass Harp* opens on Broadway.
1954	Mother commits suicide in January. In Italy for filming of his script *Beat the Devil*. Theatrical version of "A House of Flowers" opens on Broadway in December.
1956	*The Muses Are Heard* is published.

1958	*Breakfast at Tiffany's* is published.
1959	*Observations* is published, containing photos by Richard Avedon and commentary by Capote. Begins research for *In Cold Blood*.
1963	*The Selected Writings of Truman Capote* is published.
1966	*In Cold Blood* and *A Chrismas Memory* are published.
1967	*In Cold Blood*, the film version, is released.
1968	Publishes *The Thanksgiving Visitor*.
1971	Operated on for cancer.
1973	Publishes *The Dogs Bark: Public People and Private Places*.
1977	Father dies.
1980	Publishes *Music for Chameleons*.
1982	Joseph Capote dies.
1983	Publishes *One Christmas*.
1984	Dies on August 25 in Los Angeles.
1985	*Three* is published.
1987	*Answered Prayers: The Unfinished Novel* is published.

Contributors

HAROLD BLOOM is Sterling Professor of the Humanities at Yale University and Henry W. and Albert A. Berg Professor of English at the New York University Graduate School. He is the author of over 20 books, including *Shelley's Mythmaking* (1959), *The Visionary Company* (1961), *Blake's Apocalypse* (1963), *Yeats* (1970), *A Map of Misreading* (1975), *Kabbalah and Criticism* (1975), *Agon: Toward a Theory of Revisionism* (1982), *The American Religion* (1992), *The Western Canon* (1994), and *Omens of Millennium: The Gnosis of Angels, Dreams, and Resurrection* (1996). *The Anxiety of Influence* (1973) sets forth Professor Bloom's provocative theory of the literary relationships between the great writers and their predecessors. His most recent books include *Shakespeare: The Invention of the Human* (1998), a 1998 National Book Award finalist, *How to Read and Why* (2000), and *Genius: A Mosaic of One Hundred Exemplary Creative Minds* (2002). In 1999, Professor Bloom received the prestigious American Academy of Arts and Letters Gold Medal for Criticism, and in 2002 he received the Catalonia International Prize.

KENNETH T. REED has taught at Miami University. Aside from his book on Truman Capote he has written others as well, including *S. N. Behrman*.

ROBERT SIEGLE teaches English at Virginia Polytechnic Institute and State University. He has published a number of critical essays as well as a book entitled *Suburban Ambush: Downtown Writing and the Fiction of Insurgency*.

BRUCE BAWER has written a number of books on a range of topics, including *Prophets & Professors: Essays on the Lives & Works of Modern Poets.*

BLAKE ALLMENDINGER has published works on Shakespeare and Goldsmith. He is the author of *Ten Most Wanted: The New Western Literature.*

ERIC HEYNE teaches English at the University of Alaska, Fairbanks. He has published a number reviews and is the editor of *Desert, Garden, Margin, Range: Literature on the American Frontier.*

CHRIS ANDERSON teaches English at Oregon State University. He is the author and co-author of a number of titles. He is also the editor of *Literary Nonfiction: Theory, Criticism, Pedagogy.*

HELEN S. GARSON has taught English and American studies at George Mason University. She has written numerous essays about Truman Capote as well as two books on him. She writes and lectures in the United States and abroad about twentieth-century literature.

BRIAN CONNIFF teaches English at the University of Dayton. He has written essays on twentieth-century authors and has published *The Lyric & Modern Poetry: Olson, Creeley, Bunting.*

HORST TONN has published a book in German on documentary literature.

JOHN HOLLOWELL teaches English and comparative literature at the University of California at Irvine. He has published *Fact & Fiction: The New Journalism and the Nonfiction Novel* and numerous essays.

WILLIAM WHITE TISON PUGH has taught at the University of Oregon.

Bibliography

Algeo, Ann M. *The Courtroom as Forum: Homicide Trials by Dreiser, Wright, Capote, and Mailer.* New York: Peter Lang, 1996.

Bogh, Jens. "I: Truman Capote; II: *In Cold Blood.*" In Bogh, Jens, and Steffen Skovmand. *Six American Novels: From New Deal to New Frontier. A Workbook.* Aarhus: Akademisk Boghandel, 1972.

Bonner, Thomas, Jr. "Truman Capote." In Rubin, Louis D. Jr.; Blyden Jackson; Rayburn S. Moore; Lewis P. Simpson; Thomas Daniel Young. *The History of Southern Literature.* Baton Rouge: Louisiana State University Press, 1985.

Bonnet, Jean Marie. "Truman Capote: A Selected Bibliography," *Delta* 11 (1980): pp. 89-104.

Brown, Cecil M. "Plate du Jour: Soul Food: Truman Capote on Black Culture," *Quilt* 1 (1981): pp. 36-42.

Christensen, Peter G. "Truman Capote (1924-1984)." In Nelson, Emmanuel S. *Contemporary Gay American Novelists: A Bio-Bibliographical Critical Sourcebook.* Westport, CT: Greenwood, 1993.

Collett, Alan. "Literature, Criticism, and Factual Reporting," *Philosophy and Literature* 13, no. 2 (October 1989): pp. 282-96.

Creeger, George R. *Animals in Exile, Imagery and Theme in Capote's In Cold Blood.* Middletown, CT: Center for Advanced Studies, Wesleyan University, 1967.

173

D'Arcy, Chantal Cornut-Gentille. "Who's Afraid of the Femme Fatale in *Breakfast at Tiffany's*? Exposure and Implications of a Myth." In D'Arcy, Chantal Cornut-Gentille, and José Angel García Landa, eds. *Gender I-Deology: Essays on Theory, Fiction and Film*. Amsterdam, Netherlands: Rodopi, 1996.

Davis, Robert C. "*Other Voices, Other Rooms* and the Ocularity of American Fiction," *Delta* 11 (1980): pp. 1-14.

DeBellis, Jack. "Visions and Revisions: Truman Capote's *In Cold Blood*," *Journal of Modern Literature* 7 (1979): pp. 519-36.

Dorfel, Hanspeter. "Truman Capote, 'Master Misery' (1949)." In Hallwas, John E., and Dennis J. Reader, eds. *The Vision of this Land: Studies of Vachel Lindsay, Edgar Lee Masters, and Carl Sandburg*. Macomb: Western Illinois University Press, 1976.

Durand, Regis. "On Conversing: In/On Writing," *Sub-stance* 27 (1980): pp. 47-51.

Forward, Stephanie. "*In Cold Blood*: More Than Just an Unusual Murder Novel," *English Review* 6, no. 4 (1996): pp. 21-3.

Galloway, David. "Real Toads in Real Gardens: Reflections on the Art of Nonfiction Fiction and the Legacy of Truman Capote." In Borgmeier, Raimund, ed. *Gattungsprobleme in der anglo-amerikanischen Literatur*. Tubingen: Niemeyer, 1986.

Garrett, George. "Crime and Punishment in Kansas: Truman Capote's *In Cold Blood*," *The Hollins Critic* 3, no. 1 (1966): pp. 1-12.

Garson, Helen S. "From Success to Failure: Capote's Grass Harp," *The Southern Quarterly* 33, nos. 2-3 (Winter-Spring 1995): pp. 35-43.

———. *Truman Capote*. New York: Ungar, 1980.

Hellmann, John. "Death and Design in *In Cold Blood*: Capote's 'Nonfiction Novel' as Allegory," *Ball State University Forum* 21, no. 2 (1980): pp. 65-78.

Hersey, John. "The Legend on the License," *The Yale Review* 75, no. 2 (Winter 1986): pp. 289-314

Hicks, Jack. "'Fire, Fire, Fire Flowing Like a River, River, River': History and Postmodernism in Truman Capote's 'Handcarved Coffins.'" In D'haen, Theo and Hans Bertens, eds. *History and Post-War Writing*. Amsterdam: Rodopi, 1990.

———. *Fact & Fiction: The New Journalism and the Nonfiction Novel*. Chapel Hill: University of North Carolina Press, 1977.

Jones, Billie Louise. "The Monster in Capote," *New Orleans Review* 8, no. 1 (Winter 1981): pp. 105-106.

Keith, Don Lee. "An Interview with Truman Capote," *Contempora* 1, no. 4 (1970): pp. 36-40.

Larsen, Michael J. "Capote's 'Miriam' and the Literature of the Double," *International Fiction Review* 7 (1980): pp. 53-54.

Lodge, David. "Getting at the Truth," *Times Literary Supplement* (February 20, 1981): pp. 185-86.

McAleer, John J. "*An American Tragedy* and *In Cold Blood*," *Thought* 47 (1972): pp. 569-86.

McCord, Phyllis Frus. "The Ideology of Form: The Nonfiction Novel," *Genre: Forms of Discourse and Culture* 19, no. 1 (Spring 1986): pp. 59-79.

Mitchell-Peters, Brian. "Camping the Gothic: Que(e)ring Sexuality in Truman Capote's *Other Voices, Other Rooms*," *Journal of Homosexuality* 39, no. 1 (2000): pp. 107-38.

Nance, William L. "Variations on a Dream: Katherine Anne Porter and Truman Capote," *Southern Humanities Review* 3 (1969): pp. 338-345.

———. *The Worlds of Truman Capote*. New York: Stein and Day, 1970.

Perry, J. Douglas Jr. "Gothic as Vortex: The Form of Horror in Capote, Faulkner, and Styron," *Modern Fiction Studies* 19 (1973): pp. 153-67.

Pizer, Donald. "Documentary Narrative as Art: William Manchester and Truman Capote," *Journal of Modern Literature* 2 (1971): pp. 105-18.

Richards, Gary. "Writing the Fairy *Huckleberry Finn*: William Goyen's and Truman Capote's Genderings of Male Homosexuality," *Journal of Homosexuality* 34, no. 3 (1998): pp. 67-86.

Ruoff, Gene W. "Truman Capote: The Novelist as Commodity." In French, Warren, ed. *The Forties: Fiction, Poetry, Drama*. Deland, FL: Everett/Edwards, 1969.

Schorer, Mark. "McCullers and Capote: Basic Patterns." In Balakian, Nora and Charles Simmons, eds. *The Creative Present: Notes on Contemporary American Fiction*. Garden City, NY: Doubleday, 1963.

Smart, Robert A. *The Nonfiction Novel*. New York: University Press of America, 1985.

Sobieraj, Jerzy. "The Grotesque in the Fiction of Carson McCullers and Truman Capote." In Wojciech, Kalaga and Tadeusz Slawek, eds. *Discourse and Character*. Katowice, Poland: Uniwersytet Slaski, 1990.

Stanton, Robert J. *Truman Capote: A Primary and Secondary Bibliography.* Boston: Hall, 1980.

Trimmier, Dianne B. "The Critical Reception of Capote's *Other Voices, Other Rooms,*" *West Virginia University Philological Papers* 17 (1970): pp. 94-101.

Tuttle, Jon. "Glimpses of 'A Good Man' in Capote's *In Cold Blood,*" *ANQ: A Quarterly Journal of Short Articles, Notes, and Reviews* 1, no. 4 (October 1988): pp. 144-46.

Vidan, Ivo. "The Capitulation of Literature? The Scope of the 'Nonfictive Novel.'" In Thorson, James L. *Yugoslav Perspectives on American Literature: An Anthology.* Ann Arbor: Ardis, 1980.

Waldmeir, Joseph J. *The Critical Response to Truman Capote.* Westport, CT; London: Greenwood Press, 1999.

Wilson, Robert A. "Truman Capote: A Bibliographical Checklist," *American Book Collector* 1, no. 4 (1980): pp. 8-15.

Woodward, Robert H. "Thomas Wolfe: Truman Capote's 'Textbook,'" *The Thomas Wolfe Newsletter* 2, no. 1 (1978): p. 21.

Zacharias, Lee. "Living the American Dream: 'Children on their Birthdays,'" *Studies in Short Fiction* 12 (1975): pp. 343-50.

Acknowledgments

"Three Novel-Romances" from *Truman Capote*, by Kenneth T. Reed, G.K. Hall, © 1981, G.K. Hall. Reprinted by permission of The Gale Group.

"Capote's 'Handcarved Coffins' and the Nonfiction Novel" by Robert Siegle. From *Contemporary Literature* 25, no. 4 (Winter 1984): 437-51. © 1984 by the Board of Regents of the University of Wisconsin System. Reprinted by permission.

"Capote's Children" by Bruce Bawer. From *The New Criterion* 3, no. 10 (June 1985): 39-44. © 1985 by The Foundation for Cultural Review, Inc. Reprinted by permission.

"The Room Was Locked, With the Key on the Inside: Female Influence in Truman Capote's 'My Side of the Matter'" by Blake Allmendinger. From *Studies in Short Fiction* 24, no. 3 (Summer 1987): 279-88. © 1987 by Blake Allmendinger. Reprinted by permission of author.

"Toward a Theory of Literary Nonfiction" by Eric Heyne. From *Modern Fiction Studies* 33, no. 3 (Autumn 1987): 479-90. © 1987 by the Purdue Research Foundation. Reprinted by permission.

"Fiction, Nonfiction, and the Rhetoric of Silence: The Art of Truman Capote" by Chris Anderson. From *Midwest Quarterly* 28, no. 3 (Spring 1987): 340-53. © 1987 by Pittsburg State University. Reprinted by permission.

"Those Were the Lovely Years" from *Truman Capote: A Study of Short Fiction*, by Helen S. Garson. © 1992, Twayne Publishers. Reprinted by permission of The Gale Group.

Index